Taking Action Against Corruption in Asia and the Pacific

Papers Presented at the Third ADB/OECD Conference on Combating Corruption in the Asia-Pacific Region

Tokyo, Japan
28-30 November 2001

Organisation for Economic
Co-operation and Development

Asian Development Bank

ISBN 971-561-453-1
Publication Stock No. 050202

Published by the Asian Development Bank
P.O. Box 789, 0980 Manila, Philippines

Contents

Abbreviations and Acronyms

ACPF	Asia Crime Prevention Foundation (Japan)
ADB	Asian Development Bank
BIFR	Board for Financial and Industrial Reconstruction (India)
BSE	Bombay Stock Exchange
CDF	Comprehensive Development Framework (Kyrgyz Republic)
CSO	civil society organization
DFI	development finance institution
GAP	Governance Action Plan (Cambodia)
GNP	gross national product
ICICI	Industrial Credit and Investment Corporation of India
IGEC	International Group of Experts on Corruption
OECD	Organisation for Economic Co-operation and Development
NGO	nongovernment organization
NSPR	National Strategy for Poverty Reduction (Kyrgyz Republic)
PSPD	People's Solidarity for Participatory Democracy (Republic of Korea)
SCAC	Sennan City Agricultural Cooperative (Japan)
SEBI	Securities and Exchange Board of India
SICA	Sick Industrial Companies (Special Provisions) Act (India)
SOE	state-owned enterprise
TI	Transparency International
TIN	Transparency International Nepal
UN	United Nations
UNAFEI	United Nations Asia and Far East Institute for the Prevention of Crime and the Treatment of Offenders (Japan)
UNDP	United Nations Development Programme

Foreword

Corruption can reduce a country's economic output and deprive its citizens of precious resources that could enable the poor to better their lives. With the growing awareness of this negative impact of corruption, the attitude in Asia and the Pacific toward corruption seems to be changing. Companies are more reluctant to compromise their reputations and risk heavy sanctions for paying under-the-table fees to win contracts, and governments across the region acknowledge that corruption erodes the rule of law, undermines the public's trust in government, and threatens economic and political stability.

The endorsement of the Anti-Corruption Action Plan for Asia-Pacific (see appendix II) by 17 countries from the region clearly reflects this growing trend to take concrete action against corruption in the region.[1] This joint action came at the end of the third annual conference of the Asian Development Bank/Organisation for Economic Co-operation and Development (ADB/OECD) Anti-Corruption Initiative for Asia-Pacific, hosted by the government of Japan and organized by the ADB and the OECD in November 2001 in Tokyo.

The Tokyo conference was the third annual meeting of the ADB/OECD Anti-Corruption Initiative for Asia-Pacific,[2] and brought together some 150 senior government officials of Asian and Pacific countries and representatives from the private sector, civil society, the international donor community, and academia. The conference addressed the three main areas of the Action Plan that focus on key aspects of an effective fight against corruption: (a) developing efficient and transparent systems of public service, (b) strengthening anti-bribery actions and promoting integrity in business operations, and (c) supporting active public involvement. This publication contains selected conference papers pertinent to these three themes.

Countries that endorsed the Action Plan will now begin to design their individual strategies to implement it. According to the implementation strategy

---

[1] The 17 countries that have endorsed the Action Plan are Bangladesh, Cook Islands, Fiji Islands, India, Indonesia, Japan, Republic of Korea, Kyrgyz Republic, Malaysia, Mongolia, Nepal, Pakistan, Papua New Guinea, Philippines, Samoa, Singapore, and Vanuatu. Kazakhstan joined this group of countries by endorsing the Action Plan on 22 May 2002.

[2] The two previous meetings were held in Manila in October 1999 and in Seoul in December 2000.

for the Action Plan, countries are required to identify up to three priority areas for reform under any of the plan's three pillars of action. Countries must then report on progress accomplished in relation to these actions. This takes place in the framework of the Action Plan Steering Group, which endorsing countries have established with support from the Initiative's secretariat.

Jak Jabes, advisor for governance, Regional and Sustainable Development Department, ADB; Frédéric Wehrlé, coordinator for anti-corruption initiatives, Anti-Corruption Division, Directorate for Financial, Fiscal and Enterprise Affairs, OECD; and Gretta Fenner, manager of the Anti-Corruption Initiative for Asia-Pacific, Anti-Corruption Division, Directorate for Financial, Fiscal and Enterprise Affairs, OECD, coordinated the conference on which this publication is based and represent the two organizations in the Initiative's secretariat. Consultancy services and coordination by Denis Osborne, governance and development advisor, and editing by Alice Faintich, both under contract to the ADB, and support from the OECD's Public Management Service and Centre for Co-operation with Non-Members, are gratefully acknowledged. Marilyn Pizarro, consultant to the ADB, provided research and editorial assistance, and together with Wendy Prince, administrative assistant in the OECD's Anti-Corruption Division, handled the logistical arrangements for the Tokyo conference.

The views expressed in this publication do not necessarily reflect those of the ADB's Board and member countries or of the OECD and its member countries. It is published jointly by the ADB's Regional and Sustainable Development Department and by the OECD's Directorate for Financial, Fiscal and Enterprise Affairs.

AKIRA SEKI
Director General, Regional and Sustainable Development Department, ADB

WILLIAM WITHERELL
Director, Directorate for Financial, Fiscal and Enterprise Affairs, OECD

Executive Summary

Experience from the Asia-Pacific region has shown that corruption harms a country's economy, undermines the rule of law, and weakens public trust in government. Given their dependence on public services, the poor are the hardest hit. Studies have shown that corruption can cost the equivalent of 17 percent of a country's gross domestic product, robbing the population of resources that could be used to reduce poverty and promote sustainable development.

To counter this destructive impact of corruption on their economies and on social stability, 17 participating countries of the Asian Development Bank/Organisation for Economic Co-operation and Development (ADB/OECD) Anti-Corruption Initiative for Asia-Pacific have endorsed an Anti-Corruption Action Plan for Asia-Pacific.[1] This joint action came at the end of the Initiative's third annual conference in November 2001, held in Tokyo, hosted by the government of Japan and organized by the ADB and the OECD with the support of the Initiative's partners, including the Department for International Development of the United Kingdom, the Pacific Basin Economic Council, Transparency International, and the United Nations Development Programme.

The call to develop a comprehensive set of actions against corruption was made at the Initiative's previous annual conference held in Seoul in December 2000. The text as endorsed in Tokyo results from an intensive drafting process by governments in the region and experts from civil society, the business sector, and the international donor community. As such, the Action Plan reflects shared concerns and aims of all stakeholders from Asia and the Pacific and builds upon the in-depth discussions between participants of the ADB/OECD Initiative in recent years. Its endorsement at the Tokyo conference is viewed as an important step in achieving concrete anti-corruption action and proves the region's strong commitment to the fight against corruption and to a regional and action-oriented approach.

---

[1] The countries that have endorsed the Action Plan are Bangladesh, Cook Islands, Fiji Islands, India, Indonesia, Japan, Republic of Korea, Kyrgyz Republic, Malaysia, Mongolia, Nepal, Pakistan, Papua New Guinea, Philippines, Samoa, Singapore, and Vanuatu. Kazakhstan became the 18th country to endorse the Action Plan on 22 May 2002. Other ADB member countries from Asia and the Pacific are invited to endorse the Action Plan. See Appendix II for the text of the Action Plan.

The agenda of the Tokyo conference aimed to support endorsing countries in defining their individual Action Plan implementation strategies by addressing key issues under the Plan's three pillars of action: Promotion of Accountable and Reliable States (Session II); Preventive and Enforcement Measures to Fight Bribery (Session III); and Strengthening Civic Participation (Session IV). Two parallel focus groups in each session sought to identify specific remedies for major problems in these areas as identified by participants in the Initiative. Results of the focus group discussions are expected to have a direct impact on anti-corruption reform efforts undertaken to implement the Action Plan. This publication presents a number of the oral and written contributions to these discussions.

MAJOR CHALLENGES AND THEIR SOLUTIONS

In the opening session speakers from Australia, Cambodia, and Nepal summarized a number of challenges that Asian and Pacific countries are facing in their fight against corruption. These range from coalition building efforts to further involve civil society in the fight against corruption and the donor community's role in helping countries establish central anti-corruption bodies and develop a national anti-corruption strategy, to undertaking public administration reforms in situations of economic and political instability. The aim of the opening session was to discuss how the proposed Action Plan could contribute to finding solutions to these kinds of challenges.

In this context the paper by Sum Manit, Cambodia's secretary of state, highlights the need to take a country's historical context into account when developing country-specific programs to tackle corruption, and to follow a holistic approach that provides for preventive as well as enforcement measures. Similarly, the paper by Barry O'Keefe, a supreme court judge in New South Wales, Australia, emphasizes that the primary responsibility for anti-corruption reform resides within countries. At the same time, and based on the long experience of assistance provided by the Australian government, his paper discusses the complementary role of the donor community in supporting anti-corruption efforts by countries in the region. The paper presented by Devendra Raj Panday, president of Transparency International Nepal, underlines the crucial but complex, and sometimes ambiguous, role of nongovernment organizations (NGOs) in the fight against corruption and, consequently, the urgent need to implement pillar III of the Action Plan.

Regarding the role of the Action Plan in solving some of these challenges, the participants agreed that it was a timely and welcome instrument that offers useful guidelines, and that its implementation mechanisms promised to produce some tangible outcomes.

Following the overview on the current situation in the region, the participants split up into smaller working groups to address specific measures proposed by the Action Plan that could help overcome some of the challenges evoked in the opening session.

PROMOTING RELIABLE AND ACCOUNTABLE STATES

Accountable and reliable public services inspire public trust and create a favorable environment for businesses, and hence contribute to the functioning of markets and to economic growth. Public servants who serve the public interest fairly and reliably and who manage public resources properly are a prerequisite for public trust in government and a keystone of good governance. The papers presented in this session discussed specific tools to ensure accountable and transparent public administration, namely, the disclosure of public servants' assets and interests and the enforcement of rules governing transparency in politics.

Disclosure of Information

Access to relevant information by citizens, and thus the disclosure of such information by the state, are key conditions for transparency in public service and for citizens to trust and be involved in public affairs. Disclosure of information about public officials' personal interests, for example, is a powerful tool for avoiding conflicts of interest. Similarly, the disclosure of their personal assets and liabilities is an important prerequisite for ensuring the proper use of public resources, and thus for a more effective fight against corruption. In many countries, however, citizens encounter difficulties when trying to access such information, and governments are reluctant to release certain information. This is often because the laws governing access to information are unclear or nonexistent. Furthermore, even when such laws are on the books their enforcement is frequently insufficient, sometimes because it implies profound changes to the traditional operation of public services.

The media have a major role to play in facilitating the public's access to information. The paper by Zohra Yusuf from the Human Rights Commission of Pakistan shows how the legacy of Pakistan's past, that is, the nondisclosure of information that traditionally reigns in the military and the struggles between political parties, has instilled a culture of nondisclosure of information in Pakistan. The absence of a legal framework governing access to and disclosure of information has made the media the primary source of information, a fact that even Pakistan's superior courts have acknowledged in a number of corruption investigations involving high-ranking officials. While the author concludes with a list of recommendations for any government's attempt to establish a meaningful freedom of information law, she also stresses that any such law can only be effective if it is supported and understood by the citizenry at large and by free media.

The late entry into force of an access to information law in Japan (April 2001) has a somewhat different background, as highlighted in the paper by Akira Yamada from the Information Disclosure Review Board of Japan. Two main factors seem to have contributed to the passage of this law. First, competition between political parties in 1993, when for the first time in many years a new party took over the government, seems to have accelerated the development of an access to information law. Second, the author argues that the exposure of wrongdoing in Japan's public service, mainly by the media since the mid-1980s, has made the general public more critical about the work of the public administration, and hence the call for more accountability and transparency.

Yet implementation of this law continues to suffer from a number of problems, including the difficulty of clearly defining the notion of accountability, which consequently makes the concept hard to understand for both the public and civil servants who have to implement this principle. Furthermore, implementation of the law is hindered by a shortage of human resources and problems linked to conflicts between the protection of personal information and sufficient disclosure of administrative information. Nevertheless, overall the law has contributed to changes in the attitude and mentality in public administration, both positively and negatively. Public officials seem to have a greater sense of responsibility and to be more inclined to keep a spirit of accountability in mind when doing their work; however, they now also tend to avoid documenting delicate issues or innovative proposals so as not to expose themselves to possible public exposure or criticism.

The establishment and enforcement of an adequate and effective information disclosure policy in the ADB had to cope with similar challenges as those its member countries experienced. While recognizing that only the greatest possible degree of transparency and accountability in its activities can ensure the success of ADB's mission, legal and practical constraints continue to pose problems. To ensure free and frank discussion with its member countries, confidentiality is often an important prerequisite, and the efficiency in releasing classified information often suffers from the need to request authorization from authors or other parties that legally own the copyright to certain documents. The paper by Clay Wescott explains the mechanisms that ADB has put in place to overcome some of these challenges and underlines that the most important preconditions for effective implementation of information disclosure rules include education, constant dialogue between concerned parties, and the use of modern communication technologies.

Promoting Integrity in Politics

Integrity in politics is a major problem in most countries and nontransparent political financing has been at the root of many recent large-scale corruption scandals both within and outside the Asia-Pacific region. In established democracies political corruption contributes to growing disillusionment with democratic processes. In emerging democracies it poses an even greater threat to the sustainability of democratic institutions. To reduce political corruption and strengthen accountability in government, the relevant rules should strive for a high degree of disclosure and regulation of political financing with at least minimal standards of transparency.

Lim Guan Eng, a former member of Parliament from Malaysia, addressed a number of issues arising from money politics, political patronage, and conflicts of interest caused by the narrow links between political parties and corporations in Malaysia. Political leadership and political will, transparency and accountability with clear rules as to the full and free disclosure of information, public declaration of personal assets, and open invitations to public scrutiny are extremely important in this context. An independent judicial system based on the rule of law is also a crucial prerequisite, as illustrated by recurrent failures of enforcement of the relevant laws in Malaysia and elsewhere in the region.

Remedies to these challenges do exist, however. The lack of enforcement of relevant laws needs to be countered by further strengthening of the judiciary, the police, and independent regulatory bodies; political will and more public trust in government and public services can be fostered by the existence of a strong political opposition and healthy democratic processes in government as well as in political parties; and inadequate access to information and insufficient understanding of disclosed information by citizens can be countered by education targeted at all levels of society and the involvement of citizens in governmental processes.

The question of whether the OECD Anti-Bribery Convention provides additional mechanisms to prohibit the bribery of political parties and party officers and other forms of influence raised much interest among the participants. The answer to the question is yes and no. In some legal systems definitions of "political party" and "party officer" are vague and the assimilation of these notions with the concept of "public official" is difficult; however, the convention does cover some acts of bribery involving these people, for instance, if a political party officer also happens to be a public official or if he or she acts as an intermediary between the briber and the public official. Furthermore, if the bribery transaction takes place between the briber and the public official, but the political party and the party officer are the beneficiaries, the convention can still be applied to punish the bribe payer. Nevertheless, this leaves important gaps for which the paper by Enery Quinones, head of OECD's Anti-Corruption Division, seeks to identify a number of solutions.

PREVENTIVE AND ENFORCEMENT MEASURES TO FIGHT BRIBERY

Another issue addressed at the Tokyo conference dealt with the question of how to prevent corruption in business and how to sanction such practices where they occur. In this context the participants discussed two separate but related tools, first, improving (compliance with) corporate governance standards; and second, enhancing law enforcement mechanisms for dealing with bribery in business transactions.

Corporate Governance and Compliance Schemes

Understanding is growing that the basic responsibility for preventing and detecting corruption in business operations resides with company management. Key management functions include (a) monitoring and managing potential conflicts of interest by management, board members, and shareholders; (b) ensuring the integrity of the corporation's accounting and financial reporting systems; and (c) monitoring the effectiveness of the governance practices under which the firm operates. Against this background, the participants discussed successes and challenges of current approaches by policymakers and market participants in the region and categories and modes of governance using India and Japan as examples. The report from India focuses on external factors that have influenced the development of corporate governance, while the report from Japan concentrates on internal factors.

The paper by Omkar Goswami of the Confederation of Indian Industries argues that while corporate governance has been slow in making its mark in India, the next few years are likely to see progress in this regard because of Indian corporations' extensive and growing exposure to competitors from the industrial countries. The opportunity to attract foreign investment grows if governance standards are improved, and the arrival of relatively young, modern, outward-oriented professionals at the top of new companies is further contributing to the establishment of higher standards in corporate India. In addition to these external factors, the media, in particular the financial press, and public opinion have increasingly been playing an important role in encouraging the private sector to enhance its corporate governance policy.

In Japan factors inherent to Japanese social and economic culture have had a stronger impact on the development of corporate governance. Yoichiro Hamabe, partner at the law firm of Hamabe and Matsumoto in Japan, explains that preferential treatment granted to so-called "professional shareholders" and scandal that have often involved these professional shareholders in recent years have encouraged many companies to consider implementing internationally recognized principles of corporate governance and adopting compliance schemes. In developing such instruments, however, a number of questions arose in the specific context of the Japanese economy, namely, whether the adoption of another country's or culture's model can be sufficiently adapted to the specific economic structure in Japan, or what impact the erosion of the lifetime employment system might have on Japan's corporate structures. Issues related to the general role of shareholders also need attention, as well as the question of how to separate decisionmaking responsibilities from executing bodies.[2]

During the subsequent discussion the participants observed that even if companies subscribed to the sophisticated corporate governance policies inherent in international codes and standards, for example, in relation to accounting rules, niches for bribe payments or interest-driven party contributions continue to exist. They also raised concerns about possibly

---

[2] An unedited version of this paper can be found at http://www1.oecd.org/daf/ASIAcom/publications.htm.

corrupt or understaffed judiciaries that would impede the effective enforcement of relevant laws and regulations, and about the overwhelming power of multinational enterprises that many suspected of applying double standards, that is, one at home and another abroad. They considered the OECD's work on combating bribery of foreign public officials in international business transactions to be a good approach to convincing companies to change their attitudes in this regard.

The Role of the Judiciary: Improving the Investigation and Prosecution of Bribery

All countries of the region have made bribery of domestic public officials a criminal offense, and this extends to bribery of foreign officials from states that are signatories of the OECD Bribery Convention and a few other countries such as Singapore.[3] Despite these positive achievements, many countries have found prosecuting such offenses hard because of weak coordination between law enforcement agencies, slow cooperation with foreign jurisdictions, and lack of adequate enforcement resources.

The study presented by Narayanan Srinivasan from Edith Cowan University in Australia illustrates similar perceptions in the Australian and Indonesian police forces with respect to effective investigation of corruption, signaling that regional cooperation in relation to training investigative bodies can be mutually beneficial and can contribute to better international cooperation in such matters. His study also finds a number of differences between Western and Asian approaches to investigating and prosecuting corruption, with the former being perceived as focusing on processes rather than outcomes, and the author stresses that processes need to be kept as simple as possible to avoid creating opportunities for additional corrupt behavior. In this context the question arises whether the process or the outcome of an investigation and prosecution of corruption is more important, hence whether being "accountably corrupt" can be accepted as long as the process is being followed, or whether ethical and moral issues should play a role as well.

Questions related to investigative procedures are also addressed in the paper by Yuichiro Tachi from Japan about the role of Japan's public prosecutors in enforcing anti-corruption legislation. One of the major

---

[3] Countries from the Asia-Pacific region that have ratified the OECD Anti-Bribery Convention are Australia, Japan, Republic of Korea, and New Zealand.

problems prosecutors encounter is linked to provisions for criminal immunity for witnesses. Major cases such as the Lockheed case highlight that the Japanese Code of Criminal Procedure does not sufficiently provide for an efficient and fair application of criminal immunity. The paper therefore argues for the need to modify Japanese legislation to introduce new investigative techniques, including provisions that permit prosecutors to offer immunity in return for evidence, and states that this might happen as a result of Japan's ratification of the United Nations Convention Against Transnational Organized Crime.

The paper by Gerald Sumida, ADB general counsel, also looks at issues pertaining to enforcement. While adequate anti-corruption rules and legislation are in place in most countries, enforcement poses serious problems. The Asia-Pacific region faces a number of specific challenges in this regard, including a shortage of skilled and equipped investigators and the lack of clear separation between and within the judicial system, the police administration, the investigative and prosecutorial administration, and other parts of the government structure involved in law enforcement and the administration of justice. Addressing these problems requires that comprehensive judicial reform efforts are put in a much broader societal context centered around strengthening of the rule of law in general, and therefore focus on increasing the public's respect for the rule of law and the legal order. Without full public and political support and without recognizing that judicial reform needs to be placed in a long-term perspective, any reform effort will fall short of its goals.

The concerns raised by Narayanan Srinivasan, Yuichiro Tachi, and Gerald Sumida were shared by the participants, who during the subsequent discussion focused on possible remedies, such as the need for appropriate training and clear formal guidelines for pertinent personnel, the need for greater public awareness, and the importance of protecting those willing to cooperate with investigative authorities.

STRENGTHENING CIVIC PARTICIPATION IN THE FIGHT AGAINST CORRUPTION

Attacking the problem of corruption calls for deep social change, which cannot take place without the involvement and support of civil society organizations. To ensure such involvement, governments need to take proactive steps, and continuous capacity building within NGOs, the private sector, and the media is necessary to ensure that their anti-corruption actions remain effective.

Government-NGO Interaction

A prerequisite for effective collaboration between governments and civil society is both parties' acknowledgment of the value added of such collaboration. Furthermore, such collaboration has to result in concrete outcomes if it is not to remain as simple lip service.

Experience in the Kyrgyz Republic, presented by Tolondu Toichubaev from the Corporate Technologies Center, shows that efficient collaboration between governments and NGOs often suffers from a lack of understanding and acceptance on the part of governments of the value added of national anti-corruption coalitions that involve various social partners. Under such conditions NGOs must receive the necessary support for capacity building to enable them to actively promote and foster such coalitions.

In the Republic of Korea, as illustrated in the paper by Taeho Lee of the People's Solidarity for Participatory Democracy, the involvement of civil society organizations in government activities has recently gained in acceptance. . The campaign for meaningful anti-corruption legislation since 1996 by the People's Solidarity for Participatory Democracy and other NGOs has significantly changed attitudes toward corruption in the government and among the general public, and resulted in the entry into force of Korea's Anti-Corruption Law in 2002. The paper showcases a number of ways in which NGOs can run such a campaign, for example, by submitting petitions to the government, holding public discussions and running street campaigns, collecting signatures, and collaborating with the media.

The subsequent discussion in the focus group raised the problem of NGOs' independence, given that they often rely on funding from the state or from international donors, and the need to monitor NGOs in relation to their own transparency. Furthermore, the participants addressed the reluctance of both governments and NGOs to cooperate if one perceives the other to be hostile or critical, and the dilemma that this causes given that a certain level of criticism is acknowledged to be healthy for a productive relationship between the two.

Society in Action Against Corruption

Many governments in the Asia-Pacific region have recently engaged in reforming the legal and organizational infrastructure for instilling transparency and accountability in governance. Laws have been passed and specialized anti-corruption bodies have been created. Yet corruption continues to be rampant, and top political leaders and judges have been charged with corruption and cronyism. Under these circumstances the demand for and recourse to civil society measures for enhancing transparency and accountability is increasing. Such measures can include lifestyle checks, civil society watchdog organizations, report cards, and integrity pacts.

Minoru Shikita from the Asian Crime Prevention Foundation analyzes the successes and failures of the fight against corruption in Asia, with a specific spotlight on civil society action in Japan. The author concludes that some of the important tasks of NGOs in supporting anti-corruption efforts by governments are to reflect on innovative and effective legal and criminal justice mechanisms, to promote best practices, to encourage and monitor the impartiality of investigations, and to strengthen preventive measures throughout government and society.

The paper by Gopakumar Krishnan gives an example of such targeted action by NGOs. The Public Affairs Centre in Bangalore has engaged in reflections about how to improve access to information with the aim of increasing political participation by civil society. A key task to be solved in this context relates to how to ensure the quality of information as opposed to its quantity. Major steps to be taken include challenging discretionary abuse by the state and the opaqueness of political party financing and entering the difficult terrain of "contested information". The paper presents a number of specific actions to enhance proper enforcement of access to information laws or, in the absence of an adequate legal framework, to promote the establishment of such a framework.

Framework for Action

After concluding presentations by the government of Japan, representatives from civil society (Transparency International), the private sector (the Pacific Basic Economic Council), and the international donors' community (Department for International Development of the United Kingdom), and the Initiative's secretariat, 17 countries from the Asia-Pacific region that were participating in the Tokyo conference endorsed the Anti-Corruption Action Plan for Asia-Pacific. The endorsing statements clearly expressed the countries' strong commitment to take concrete and action-oriented steps to enhance their fight against corruption and to cooperate in these efforts in the framework of the Action Plan.[4]

---

[4] The endorsing statements can be found in the Action Plan pamphlet published in March 2002 by ADB and OECD, and at http://www.oecd.org/daf/ASIAcom/ActionPlan.htm.

In a next step, based on the Implementation Plan of the Action Plan, the endorsing countries identified up to three priority areas for reform under any of the Plan's three pillars of action. The countries discussed this first set of priority areas for reform and corresponding implementation projects in May 2002 in Manila. Officials at the meeting reported on and reviewed initial reforms envisaged or already taken to comply with the Action Plan, including training investigation and prosecution authorities to ensure the proper enforcement of relevant laws; clarifying and, if required, amending existing legislation on corporate governance; providing integrity training programs for civil servants; implementing new systems to protect whistle-blowers; and launching public awareness campaigns in cooperation with civil society organizations. Most of the selected reform areas reflect discussions held at the Tokyo conference.

The endorsing countries will meet again in early 2003 for a first assessment of the concrete impact of these measures and to consider additional legislative and enforcement actions. Through the Initiative's web site, and in the framework of the follow-up meeting to the Tokyo conference, endorsing countries' achievements in implementing the Action Plan will be shared with a larger public, including interested representatives from civil society, the private sector, and the international donor community.

Welcoming Remarks

Shomei Yokouchi

Ladies and gentlemen, distinguished participants, in my capacity as senior vice-minister of justice, whereby I am responsible for all matters related to the Ministry of Justice, including planning criminal legislation to deal with corruption, and also on behalf of the government of Japan, I would like to convey to all of you participating in this conference my heartfelt welcome.

Corruption clandestinely erodes the sound foundations of civil society. It derails decisionmaking and policymaking, thereby impeding sound social and economic development. In this sense corruption is the most serious obstacle to democracy and sustainable development.

Complete freedom from corruption is difficult for any country to achieve. The fight against corruption has now become an international issue, and the search for ways to tackle this malaise has resulted in many initiatives being taken on a global level. Today here in Tokyo, representatives from Asia-Pacific countries are assembled to show their collective will to eradicate corruption. This clearly testifies to the region's determination to join in the global efforts against corruption. Eradicating corrupt practices may not be an easy task; however, given a strong and steadfast political will, it is not an impossible one.

In response to growing awareness about the problem of corruption, the OECD and the ADB have been playing an important role in this field. Their successes include the December 2000 Conference on Combating Corruption in the Asia-Pacific Region held in Seoul, Republic of Korea. The baton has been passed from Seoul to Tokyo. Therefore we should take further, steady steps to build confidence that corruption cannot survive our collaborative efforts to eliminate it.

Let me assure all our colleagues gathered here that the government of Japan is willing to align itself with you to reinforce our fight against corruption by strengthening the rule of law and justice throughout the region. To this end we will continuously participate in this initiative.

The success of this conference depends on you. Your active involvement in and contribution to the discussion will be of vital importance in seeking effective and practical measures against corruption in the Asia-Pacific region.

In concluding, let me reiterate my sincere hope that this conference will result in success and with your cooperation will establish a cornerstone of anti-corruption strategy in the region.

Keynote Address

Toshio Kojima

Excellencies, ladies, and gentlemen: I would like to join Vice-Minister Yokouchi in extending my heartfelt welcome to all of you.

I am pleased to see the solidarity among Asian-Pacific countries in addressing a serious challenge: combating corruption. I would like to commend the regional partners, as well as the ADB and OECD, for their efforts and dedication. This conference gives momentum to our achievements to date.

At the first and second conferences in Manila and Seoul we examined "best policy measures" taken in the Asia-Pacific region, and we also discussed how we could most effectively apply such anti-corruption measures in this region. Through these discussions we have been able to achieve a greater understanding that corruption has been an obstacle to economic and social development, and that in the face of strengthening economic globalization, the continued presence of corruption in any given country should be addressed not as a national issue, but as a global one. This is because the existence of corruption anywhere could hinder efforts by international society to achieve sound development on a global scale. We have also come to share the view that if we wish to succeed in our fight against corruption, we must establish a chain of collaboration among the players—public officials, business communities, civil societies, and international organizations—in addition to enforcing legal measures.

We are now entering a new stage: taking action. In this regard I am pleased to note that the Asia-Pacific countries have taken initial anti-corruption measures. Japan, for its part, is pursuing its role domestically by enacting the National Public Service Ethics Law, and internationally by ratifying and implementing the OECD Convention on Combating Bribery of Foreign Public Officials and participating in the ongoing negotiations on the United Nations Convention against Corruption.

The important mission of this conference is to encourage all the participants to renew their determination to tackle the eradication of corruption head on and to pursue concrete actions. To propel this unique initiative forward, the conference will include discussions of the regional Anti-Corruption Action Plan, prepared by the expert group in consultation with the region's countries. The Action Plan details the primary actions with a focus on three pillars: (a) effective and transparent public services, (b) effective anti-bribery actions and corporate responsibility, and (a) active public involvement. Each pillar specifies concrete measures that will provide us with a guide to developing our own strategies.

I hope that the conference will inspire discussions leading to the endorsement of the Action Plan on Friday. Then, by implementing the Action Plan, we can demonstrate our firm determination to work toward the ambitious goal of strengthening a reliable, transparent, and competitive economic system, thereby recharging the growth engine of the Asia-Pacific region while encouraging the inflow of foreign direct investment. This bold initiative will surely lead us to our long-awaiting goal: making the 21st century the century of the Asia-Pacific region.

Opening Remarks

Seiichi Kondo

Your Excellencies, distinguished guests, it is an honor for me to welcome you to Tokyo for the third annual conference of the Asian Development Bank/Organisation for Economic Co-operation and Development (ADB/OECD) Anti-Corruption Initiative for Asia-Pacific.

I would like to take this opportunity to thank the ADB for its excellent collaboration in the organization of this conference and our other joint projects undertaken in the framework of the ADB/OECD Initiative. I would also like to extend our sincere gratitude to the government of Japan for hosting this event and to the Initiative's partner organizations, which include the Department for International Development of the United Kingdom, the Pacific Basin Economic Council, the United Nations Development Programme, and the World Bank. The support and advice of these institutions and individuals has contributed significantly to this conference.

The presence of so many key players, experts, and leaders from across the Asian and Pacific region, as well as from OECD countries and international organizations, attests to the importance of the issues that we are here to discuss. Through continuous dialogue between the private and public sectors, governments and civic organizations, and countries both within and outside the region, we are not only advancing the fight against corruption, but also building mutual understanding and confidence while learning from each other's experience. I am therefore extremely pleased to see that, as with the two previous conferences—in Manila in 1999 and Seoul in 2000—this year's annual conference of the ADB/OECD Initiative has again become a rallying point for Asian and Pacific leaders eager to curb corruption.

WHY DOES TAKING A STAND AGAINST CORRUPTION MATTER?

We all know that corruption undermines social and economic development. We know that it poses a serious threat to the development and preservation of democratic institutions. We acknowledge that corruption distorts the allocation of resources. Political leaders around the world recognize the importance and urgency of combating corruption. Observing the progress many countries of Asia and the Pacific have made is encouraging, particularly in their efforts to increase people's understanding of the negative impacts of corruption and in raising awareness of the need to combat it. In recent years governments have launched various anti-corruption programs, many of them in close collaboration with nongovernment actors. Actions to combat corruption are on the rise throughout the region.

However, we are far from having won the battle. Corruption remains pervasive throughout much of the world. Today, knowledge and awareness must be combined with political will to achieve an impact through more concrete action. Seen from this perspective, we clearly still have much to do. The ADB/OECD Initiative can continue to contribute to the strengthening of these efforts.

THE ORGANISATION FOR ECONOMIC CO-OPERATION AND DEVELOPMENT

The development of one of the world's most important anti-bribery instruments—the OECD Convention on Combating Bribery of Foreign Public Officials in International Business Transactions—shares a similar history with your efforts in Asia and the Pacific. After analyzing the nature of corruption in international business practices, OECD countries reached consensus on developing a framework for more effective action. Thus in 1997, 29 OECD countries and 5 nonmembers signed the OECD Anti-Bribery Convention. Since that time almost all the signatories have transposed it into national law. Today, the convention contributes to prevailing high standards for anti-bribery legislation and encourages meaningful preventive measures. As such, it is one of the most effective international anti-bribery tools currently in force.

ADB/OECD ANTI-CORRUPTION INITIATIVE FOR ASIA-PACIFIC: DEVELOPING A REGIONAL ACTION PLAN

Last year at this forum, representatives of more than 30 Asian and Pacific countries expressed their wish to accelerate their efforts and signaled their readiness to undertake concrete and coordinated action. The Anti-Corruption Action Plan for Asia-Pacific is the response to this demand.

The Action Plan has two main objectives: (a) to give a decisive impetus to the fight against corruption in the Asian and Pacific region; and (b) to focus anti-corruption actions on key priority areas in each country, while following a common approach and a joint agenda. To this end the Action Plan proposes a comprehensive set of actions structured according to three pillars:

- Pillar I: developing effective and transparent systems for public management
- Pillar II: strengthening anti-bribery actions and promoting integrity in business operations
- Pillar III: supporting active public involvement.

While the Action Plan is not a legally binding instrument, it is a commitment at the highest political level to tackle corruption. It sets out principles and standards for policy reform under each of its three pillars of action. By endorsing the proposed Action Plan, participating countries in the region will commit to undertaking legal and institutional reforms that aim to diminish opportunities for corruption and increase transparency and accountability in the public and private sectors.

Implementation will be designed in a manner that takes account of the diversity of cultures and economic and political systems in the region. Each participating country will be invited to identify priority areas under the three pillars for which it will then determine its reform strategies. The international donor community, the private sector, civil society, and other partners are expected to support the Asian and Pacific countries in these efforts in various ways.

Eleven of the region's countries have answered the call to jointly develop a draft Action Plan and have actively participated in two ADB/OECD expert meetings that served this purpose. Many others have provided expertise and expressed their support. In addition to countries from the region, a number of key actors from the international community, bilateral aid agencies, and civil society were involved in this process. The text that will be proposed for endorsement on the last day of this conference is thus the result of an intensive consultation process with and between governments and other actors in the region. As such, it reflects the combined ideas of these stakeholders on how to design and engage in concrete actions against corruption.

Later this morning participants will discuss the Action Plan in more detail. The different plenary sessions and focus groups will produce helpful input for countries in focusing on their anti-corruption strategies.

CONCLUSION

Let me conclude by saying that the Action Plan is a unique instrument in this region. It is the result of active and constructive dialogue with and between governments and all other partners involved in the fight against corruption in the region. As such, it combines, in a comprehensive manner, the needs and wishes of all key stakeholders.

The Action Plan is based on three principles that are, in my view, key to a successful fight against corruption: cooperation, coordination, and country ownership. I am certain that it will make an important contribution in the transition from analysis to action.

I would like to express my sincere appreciation to all those that have been involved in the development of the Action Plan for their valuable contributions, in particular, the countries that have worked together in a cooperative and effective manner.

I hope that this conference will indeed guide us toward well-targeted and concrete actions. By further enhancing our knowledge and understanding of the problems underlying corruption in this region, it can help all those anxious to fight corruption to do so in an effective way. I am convinced that your active participation here today will give rise to fruitful exchanges. Let us help each other to find the right solutions and hands-on responses to the new challenges in the fight against corruption.

I wish you a successful conference.

Opening Remarks

Gerald Sumida

Your Excellencies, distinguished guests, ladies and gentlemen, we are all pleased to be here in Tokyo for the Third Annual Conference of the ADB/ OECD Anti-Corruption Initiative for the Asia-Pacific Region. Let me also take this opportunity to thank the OECD for its excellent collaboration on this conference and the government of Japan for hosting this important meeting.

The OECD has long been at the forefront of the fight against bribery in international business dealings with its Convention on Combating Bribery of Foreign Public Officials in International Business Transactions. Our host, the government of Japan, has been a strong supporter of the ADB/OECD Initiative since the beginning. As we know, one of the major matters before us is the Action Plan presented to this conference. We thank all our partners for their help in preparing this plan, including Transparency International, the Pacific Basin Economic Council, the United Nations Development Programme, the Department for International Development of the United Kingdom, and the World Bank.

In a few countries, according to the Transparency International Corruption Index, corruption is virtually absent. These countries have extremely productive economies and their citizens enjoy high standards of living, with little or no corruption. We know that strong and transparent institutions are key to high standards of living. These societies have become prosperous because economic and social incentives reward peoples' productivity based on their skills and creativity.

However, recognizing that a corruption-free environment is primarily the result of affirmative efforts to reduce, if not eliminate, opportunities for corruption is important. Strong laws and effective police and judicial systems are essential elements of such an environment. But economies fundamentally work because of institutions that provide strong incentives for individuals and society as a whole to adhere to society's rules.

Combating corruption requires strong and enduring political commitment and leadership. The political leadership can send important signals that corruption is not tolerated. I could cite numerous approaches and proposals; however, much of this is incorporated in the Action Plan, which I urge you to review in detail.

From the ADB's standpoint, I am pleased to share with you a brief summary of some of the ADB's most recent projects and activities in this area.

In Pakistan the ADB is providing a US$350 million loan for a program to strengthen the judiciary, as well as legal enforcement mechanisms and institutions. Among other things, the program will establish a federal judicial academy, provide better budgetary support for the judicial mandate to introduce innovations in legal education, create ombudsmen to handle public legal grievances, and establish institutions for consumer protection. The program is designed to remove the constraints that a weak legal framework and the unpredictable performance of judicial institutions in Pakistan impose on the economy.

In Nepal, an ongoing governance reform program supported by the ADB contains a significant element to reduce corruption through improved and revised legislation and compliance with audits.

In addition to providing technical and financial support to its developing member countries in their anti-corruption efforts, the ADB also

- Adopted a good governance policy in 1995
- Adopted an anti-corruption policy in 1998
- Reiterated its commitment to these policies through its long-term strategic framework adopted in 2001.

The world has changed dramatically since 11 September. The attacks on the United States have demonstrated the importance of fighting money laundering, bribery, and corruption. They underscore, in particular, the need for strong, unwavering, and broadly based commitment to combat corruption in all its pernicious forms and the importance of our joint efforts in preparing the Action Plan.

The ADB looks forward to implementing the Action Plan in cooperation with the countries that endorse it. The ADB will continue to support anti-corruption initiatives in the Asia-Pacific region through its loans and technical assistance.

Again, we would like to express our sincere appreciation to all those who have been involved in the development of the Action Plan. We also wish you the best in your coming deliberations in this vitally important challenge facing all of us.

PART 1

The Challenge of Coping with Corruption

A. Strategies in the Region
B. Disclosure of Information
C. Integrity in Politics

A. Strategies in the Region

Chapter 1

Designing a Comprehensive National Anti-Corruption Strategy in Cambodia

■ **Sum Manit**

C ambodia is a postwar country. Most of the country's intellectuals were killed or fled the country during the Khmer Rouge regime, giving rise to a human resources problem. However, thanks to Prime Minister Hun Sen's win-win policy, the last Khmer Rouge forces have joined the government, and peace has been restored. In addition, Cambodia is one of those rare countries that has successfully carried out simultaneous political, economic, and governance reforms.

More than 25 years of instability and conflicts led to a total collapse of the administrative system. This accounts for the lack of accountability and transparency in public administration and in the control of budget expenditures. Some of the management problems include weak organizational structures, insufficient monitoring of the implementation of objectives, poorly coordinated government activities, insufficient competencies, and the absence of a code of ethics.

REFORMS

To address these weaknesses of the public administration, the government has created the Supreme Council for the Reform of the State, under which seven reform councils are working in the following areas: public administration, demobilization of the armed forces, reform of the Army, finance, social sectors, legal and judiciary processes, land management.

To develop the market economy and the private sector, a fundamental priority of the government is to maintain political stability and to restore public order by establishing the rule of law. Furthermore, the government acknowledges that clear and well-established legal frameworks are of the utmost importance for creating a predictable and secure living and working environment for all citizens. The government recognizes that widespread adherence to the rule of law will result in higher confidence of civil society and the local and international business community, and that this will ultimately result in higher investment and growth for Cambodia.

Fundamental freedoms are guaranteed in Cambodia. There are no restrictions on people's freedom to establish religious groups; professional associations; or voluntary organizations with social, economic, or other purposes. The Ministry of Information has officially recorded the publication of more than 100 media publications (daily, weekly, biweekly, and monthly) in local or foreign languages. No restrictions are placed on bringing in newspapers, magazines, or any other kinds of publications from abroad.

The government is committed to enhancing the quality of governance by building healthy institutions and making government operations equitable, transparent, readily accessible, efficient, and accountable to the public. It is developing its partnership with the private sector, civil society, and nongovernment organizations in formulating public policy and drafting laws.

In July 1999 the government asked the World Bank for technical assistance for capacity building in enhancing governance and fighting corruption. In November and December 1999 a local nongovernment organization carried out diagnostic governance surveys under World Bank supervision. The Cambodia Development Research Institute undertook another study of governance issues in Cambodia with ADB funding. The final outcome, with the World Bank's assistance, was the preparation of the Governance Action Plan (GAP) that is now being successfully implemented. Given the extent of progress, the authorities are currently getting ready to update the GAP in full consultation with all stakeholders.

As part of the good governance program, the public administration will be reorganized and rationalized in order to work efficiently and effectively in support of economic and social development. The government's ambitious programs to improve governance and the management of the civil service are indicative of its political will to undertake reforms to deter corruption. However, the process of change should be in step with Cambodia's absorption capacity. It must emphasizes the use of and build on national expertise by progressively increasing public sector salaries. To accelerate the pace of reforms and, at the same time, combat corruption, the government is setting up priority mission groups, which are a core of civil servants. With technical assistance from the ADB, the World Bank, and the United Nations Development Programme, the concept is currently being finalized and is expected to be implemented in 2002. With the provision of adequate incentives and an appropriate working environment, members of priority mission groups will be subjected to stringent performance and ethical standards.

At the same time, the government is designing a mechanism to enable the introduction of a tailor-made management and remuneration regime to deal with special circumstances. This mechanism would institutionalize practices whereby a portion of the revenues generated by an agency could be reallocated to the staff of that agency (for example, staff involved with customs inspections, taxation, and forest inspections). It could also address areas where independence is important, such as in the judiciary.

Another important component of the public administration reform is decentralization. The first commune elections in Cambodia were held in February 2002. The objective was to bring public services closer to the citizens and ensure the participation of civil society in the country's social and economic development. Decentralization will also contribute to poverty alleviation. To support the policy of decentralization, the Council for Administrative Reform is preparing a master plan for the deconcentration of powers from the central administration to provinces and districts.

The obvious point for starting anti-corruption efforts is to gain an understanding of the underlying causes, loopholes, and incentives that feed corrupt practices. A strategy needs to address not only enforcement and prosecution, but also prevention and community education. A strategy that focuses only on enforcement is almost certain to fail. In addition, it is axiomatic that a law enforcement approach will work only when a functioning and independent judicial system is place. To this end the government is reforming the judiciary.

ANTI-CORRUPTION ACTION PLAN

Cambodia applauds the efforts of the group of experts and ADB and OECD specialists in drafting the comprehensive Anti-Corruption Action Plan for the Asia-Pacific Region. The impression gained is that the group of experts involved largely represents an exhaustive cross-section of industrial countries and major international donors. While the document is exhaustive in describing the pillars of actions and outlining principles and standards to guide their implementation, it is silent on the level, nature, and quality of means to be made available to countries that voluntarily commit to implementing the Action Plan. In particular, it does not distinguish among countries based on their level of development and available means. All signatories are considered equals to be subjected to the same oversight and auditing regardless of their capabilities. Donors are only to endeavor to provide the necessary assistance, while participating countries are expected to commit to the Action Plan not knowing ahead of time the extent of resources likely to be at their disposal and to submit to stringent, transparent monitoring.

A number of general comments follow:

- The government's will to fight corruption does not need to be further demonstrated. It was the first government in the region to commission a survey on corruption and to act upon it. Its approach is holistic and comprehensive.
- Through the GAP the government is already committed to a comprehensive effort to curb corruption along lines similar to those proposed by the draft Action Plan by addressing the causes of corruption. Already, a number of suggested actions under each of the proposed pillars are under way under the aegis of the GAP.
- The government has always maintained that the pace and scope of GAP implementation will depend on available means. At the current stage in the country's development, the government is overly dependent on external technical and financial assistance.
- The next version of the GAP is expected to deal with the fight against corruption in a more explicit and targeted way. It will entail measures to deal with public officials, the public, business enterprises, watchdog agencies, and the legal and judiciary process.
- A commitment to taking action as a sovereign state is one thing; however, submitting to international oversight in the absence of clear commitments by the international community to provide the necessary assistance, particularly to the poorest countries, is something altogether different.
- The Action Plan should not supersede domestic efforts already in place.

Specific comments include the following:

- Pillar 1 — developing effective and transparent systems for public management
    - *Integrity in the civil service.* The government's strategy to rationalize the civil service addresses many of the suggested actions. Some, such as regular rotation of assignments, would be difficult to implement in the context of a career system such as that of Cambodia. Others, such as the declaration and monitoring of assets and liabilities, are under consideration.

— *Accountability and transparency.* For the most part, the proposed measures are already being actively pursued.

• Pillar 2 — strengthening anti-bribery actions and promoting integrity in business operations

— *Effective prevention, investigation, and prosecution.* The proposed actions relate primarily to the establishment and enforcement of an appropriate legal framework. At issue are enforcement capabilities, given the state of the judiciary and the early stage of the establishment of competent investigative and prosecutorial authorities, for instance, the National Audit Authority.

— *Corporate responsibilities and accountability.* The government has often said that it wants to encourage its partners to pursue good governance in the areas within their jurisdiction. The government is actively pursuing the implementation of an appropriate framework to guide the activities of the private sector, for example, by reviewing incentives for investment and normalizing accounting practices to conform to international standards.

• Pillar 3 — supporting active public involvement

— *Public discussion of corruption.* The government is already committed to disseminating the Diagnostic Study on Corruption as part of its GAP dissemination campaign. The preparation of GAP II will necessarily lead to extensive public discussions of corruption issues.

— *Access to information.* As mentioned earlier, the Cambodian media are already among the freest in the region. Access to information would be greatly facilitated through the advent of computerization

— *Public participation.* The government is already consulting extensively with all concerned in relation to public policy and good governance issues.

— *Core principles of implementation.* Countries that volunteer for the Action Plan will be subjected to rigorous and regular monitoring, but the plan is silent on the monitoring of assistance providers. The fight against corruption is an ongoing, long-term effort that will require long-term support, particularly in the case of developing countries. Whether donors are committed to such a long-term effort is not clear. Success will require much more than best intentions.

CONCLUSION

It is difficult to argue with the preamble to the Action Plan and the thrust of the pillars of action. However, successful implementation requires much more than a vague commitment to provide technical cooperation programs. Most of the proposed actions require significant financial resources and know-how, which are not readily available in the least developed countries. More clarification and discussion are needed before the government commits to the principles of implementation of the proposed Action Plan. For one, all countries cannot be lumped together, and the Action Plan should explicitly recognize the special circumstances of the least developed countries in the region and the need for special measures to support them.

Many studies, research projects, surveys, books, seminars, and conferences supported by the ADB, the World Bank, the OECD, Transparency International, and other organizations and governments deal with the issue of corruption. Corruption is a social and global phenomenon that is not specific to developing countries. Only its severity varies from country to country. Corruption is like a cancer that flourishes where the institutions of governance are weak, and where a government's policy and regulatory regime provides scope for it. The causes of corruption are highly contextual, rooted in a country's political development, legal development, social history, bureaucratic traditions, economic conditions, and policies.

Thus strategies to combat corruption tend to vary from one country to another. The government has resolutely embarked on its fight against corruption, as demonstrated by the GAP and its strategy to rationalize the civil service. The government is looking forward to working with its partners in this most difficult of endeavors.

Chapter 2

Transparency International and Anti-Corruption Work in Nepal

■ **Devendra Raj Panday**

The fight against corruption requires building coalitions across various segments of society and across nations. Even though the state actors that make the rules, both preventive and punitive, and implement them have an important role to play, the battle is not likely to succeed without the active efforts of other segments of society, including civic groups and businesses. Thus the value of the contributions of nongovernment organizations (NGOs) and other civil society institutions and actors has to be understood in this context. This chapter discusses the emergence and role of one such organization, Transparency International Nepal, which is part of the national, as well as the global, coalition against corruption.

The international movement against corruption is based on the fact that corruption is a global phenomenon, and that in cases of grand corruption, it has transborder implications that need a commensurate response. This recognition is what has made possible the small amount of progress made in the last few years. The international coalition against corruption is expanding by the day. The World Bank, the International Monetary Fund, the ADB, and other donors and international institutions are now taking more interest than ever before in the fight against corruption. This is because, among other things, they now realize that international development efforts and the resources mobilized and used to that end are being sabotaged by this scourge that adversely affects both the growth and equity objectives of development.

Nepal stands to benefit from the ongoing developments and international cooperation provided that its leaders have the will and the wisdom to take advantage of the opportunities to rise to the occasion and seize the moment. At the other end of the spectrum, the role of civil society is also critical. Without its contribution, a democratic culture and democratic practices are not likely to take root in the country, and in the absence of democracy resources channeled for development are unlikely to produce the intended results. In addition, the anti-corruption struggle could simply fizzle out, with dishonest political leaders and corruption-friendly elements in society hijacking the democracy movement. For civil society to play its role successfully, it has to address some challenges to its legitimacy and credibility.

TRANSPARENCY INTERNATIONAL NEPAL

The Nepali chapter of Transparency International (TI), Transparency International Nepal (TIN), was established in 1995 (formally registered in 1996), two years after the international movement had been launched in Berlin. It took the organization six months to become registered, partly because the authorities did not fully understand what "transparency" meant, and might therefore have been apprehensive about what the organizers were up to. Typical of how a bureaucracy works, a TI mission from Berlin was visiting Nepal at the behest of the then government and being feted by none other than the country's prime minister at the same time that TIN was struggling to get registered as a legal entity.

Nepal has many NGOs that are engaged in supporting good governance practices, but TIN is perhaps the only one with the sole purpose of fighting corruption in the country. It has no other agenda, and in that sense is a unique organization. However, it is by no means the only civil society organization fighting against corruption in Nepal. Many other actors, both individual and institutional, are making valuable contributions to the cause. TIN believes in building coalitions among all such actors, including donors, who may share the same values and commitment to the changes that TIN seeks.

There is also another angle to the issue of which TIN's campaigners have to be aware. The existence of a number of organizations interested in anti-corruption work also presents a challenge. The challenge does not just concern technical efficiency in a competitive milieu, but TIN's credibility and sincerity. If the public cannot see concrete outcomes, TIN's credibility and legitimacy will be questioned. Obviously, this holds true for the movement as a whole, but in Nepal the challenge becomes multiplied when TIN also falls victim to the general sense of frustration and despair arising from inadequate progress in the larger public domain, including not only development and democratization, but also peace and security.

CHALLENGES

In the six years since TIN was founded the level of corruption in Nepal has probably not decreased, though TIN can take some satisfaction that the process has been started. The successes that have been achieved through the efforts of TIN and of civil society activism in general have been more or less parallel to what the movement has been able to accomplish elsewhere in much of the developing world.

First, some years ago, corruption was not seriously discussed, although abstract writings and anecdotal stories have always appeared in the media. Now this subject has firmly entered the public agenda. It has become a priority item in deliberations concerning the country's national destiny, and concerned citizens and groups are showing a keen interest in seeking solutions to the problem. The political debate and civic discourses are swamped by charges of corruption and countercharges. The newspapers and electronic media, especially some radio stations run by the private sector, are also discussing the issue. In essence, government leaders and political parties now all speak TI's language about transparency and the need to control corruption, when until a few years ago they did not even want to hear about the subject.

Second, until relatively recently donors too were not in a mood to listen to TIN's or anybody else's messages about the need to tackle corruption. Now this subject has become a principal item on their agenda. Many donors have begun to include relevant provisions in the bilateral agreements they sign with the government, specifying the government's responsibility to be alert to the possibility of corruption and to take measures to prevent it. They may not necessarily be working hand-in-hand with TIN, but TIN does serve as point for interaction and for sharing knowledge and experience for the many who are interested.

Third, politicians lacked awareness about the need for a code of conduct and the possibility of conflicts of interests as they engaged in an economically active manner in different domains of society. Now codes of conduct are being discussed everywhere, including in parliament for its members. The upper house has already adopted such a code.

Fourth, judges and other actors in the legal profession are also developing and adopting codes of conduct for themselves.

Fifth, amid charges that the law enforcement agencies were either weak or were performing at a level below their capacity because of the state's indifference to corruption, the government was forced to appoint a committee to suggest reform measures. The committee has submitted a report with wide-ranging recommendations that include measures to be taken on the legal front, on the organizational aspects of regulatory and watchdog agencies, on public personnel management, and on ensuring transparency in government. New legislation against corruption is being discussed in parliament. The fact that the bills as drafted leave much to be desired is a separate issue. TIN and other civil society actors have had the opportunity to react to them and have made some concrete suggestions for changes.

These developments indicate that the awareness building part of TIN's work has produced useful results. The distressing factor is that awareness without concrete results on the ground can be frustrating, especially when people are impatient, as all poor and exploited people are likely to be. The difficulty arises from a situation where political leaders display a sense of helplessness as to how they can contribute to anti-corruption work without sacrificing their political careers or futures. Thus civil society must take on the task not only of criticizing political leaders, but also of showing them a way out of this dilemma.

Thus a starting point is to work on society's attitudes and values, which in the end may decide how any political regime will be allowed to function. More constructive interaction between civil society and political and bureaucratic actors is needed. This has to be done by anti-corruption campaigners, not in a "holier than thou" frame of mind, but perhaps like a doctor, who has to understand how and why an addict is addicted to the vice in the first place. These are areas where we have no blueprint to follow or do-it-yourself kit to apply. The situation is made more complex by the possibility that in some areas even domestic civil society may be deficient, ethically and professionally, and thus is not always trustworthy as a healer or a guide.

If there is one factor in Nepal that makes anti-corruption campaigners look like ignorant fools, if not also hypocrites, and makes honest citizens despondent, it is the climate of immunity. The long arm of the law rarely seems to reach corrupt officials and public functionaries, who tend to get away with their corrupt acts, unrepentant about their transgressions. While discussion about what might be done about the legal framework abound, it is not only the cynics who think that simply changing the law will not make a difference. Nepal has been a society where, according to a popular adage, the law is for the common people, while relief from its bondage is a privilege of the ruling classes.

If the situation on the punitive side is unsatisfactory, the preventive side also needs work. There is plenty of scope for improving the financial management system, the system of procurement, and the methods for ensuring transparency and probity in public life. TIN and other civic society actors have been trying to contribute in these areas by offering their services to the appropriate authorities, but when the principal bottleneck is in the area of government values and norms, TIN's enthusiasm falls on infertile ground.

PROBLEMS IN CIVIL SOCIETY

Despite the dependence on the contributions of civil society in dealing with corruption, problems are also apparent within civil society that need to be taken into account and addressed, for example:

- Law abidance by citizens is at an all time low.
- People may encourage public officials to contravene rules and regulations and support corrupt practices for their own benefit.
- Everyone wants appointments, promotions, contracts, and so on, but no one wants to wait their turn.
- Every government minister, member of parliament, or other influential public leader is constantly inundated by people seeking favors who are likely to view them as hopeless, inefficient, or insensitive if their wishes are not granted, even if that means breaking the law.
- People tend to regard every problem as a personal problem, not a social issue that needs to be addressed collectively through appropriate institutional interventions and policy decisions.

TASKS FOR TIN

In view of the foregoing, TIN needs to focus on the following actions:

- Building partnerships and coalitions with other like-minded NGOs based on shared values and common objectives
- Developing substantive (program-based) networks with relevant professional organizations, for instance, the Nepal Bar Association, the Institute of Chartered Accountants, the Nepal Engineering Association, and the Nepal Medical Association, to promote professional integrity and solidarity

- Finding ways to work with donors promote reform in their own backyards and among their partners in host countries
- Disassociating from individuals and groups, national or foreign, who believe in "cultural relativism" and profess that "this is Nepal, hence anything goes"
- Recruiting allies and finding champions that support anti-corruption values, norms, and activities within and outside state institutions.

CONCLUSION

In Nepal, as in other countries of South Asia, TIN and other related NGOs and civil society agents can make critical contributions to combating corruption. They are already making some progress. However, combating corruption is also intimately related to the need to promote a democratic culture in politics and society. TI's credibility in Nepal will thus depend upon its ability to make inroads into the political realm. A rejuvenated democratic culture should reduce corruption associated with the organization of political parties, the conduct of elections, and the behavior of state institutions.

The last point needs some elaboration. Anti-corruption work can be threatening, even for those who are relatively honest. As the Nepalese say, nobody who is entrusted with authority or has acquired substantial assets can claim "to have bathed in milk." Thus one cannot be sure how the average person will perceive a whistle-blower, though needless to say, genuinely corrupt individuals will be threatened and will do all they can to discredit whistle-blowers. Thus TIN needs to find and support those willing to champion the cause of anti-corruption within their organizations.

Chapter 3

Recent Progress in the Asia-Pacific Region from an Australian Perspective

■ **Barry S. J. O'Keefe**

Both in Australia and elsewhere, efforts have been directed at defining and improving ethical standards in the public sector. In the Asian-Pacific region they have concentrated on Indonesia and Papua New Guinea; however, Australia has also undertaken an initiative in Nepal. In addition, as a member of Interpol's International Group of Experts on Corruption (IGEC), I have drafted a set of global standards for police forces and services of those countries that are members of Interpol.

AUSTRALIA

The Western Australian government has set up a Royal Commission of Inquiry into the Police Service of the State of Western Australia. Although the commission's terms of reference are directed at a particular problem, they could be extended, as was the case with a similar Royal Commission in New South Wales from 1993-1995. The hope is that the initiative in setting up the Royal Commission is indicative of a commitment on the part of the Western Australian government to improve the attitude toward ethics among the Western Australian Police Service. In New South Wales the implementation of the numerous recommendations of the Royal Commission appears to have run into some difficulties. Indications of resistance to these reforms in some sections of the New South Wales Police Service are strong and credible. As a result, the commissioner of police has terminated the commissions and services of a number of senior officers. Given the nature of industrial and employment laws in New South Wales, the commissioner's actions have been challenged in court in some instances where the removals from office occurred because the commissioner had lost confidence in the officers in question or because of what the commissioner believed to be inappropriate conduct on their part.

INDONESIA

Through the Australian Agency for International Development, the government of Australia funded an anti-corruption initiative in Indonesia that involved drafting a statute to set up an anti-corruption agency. The initiative was embraced by the then president of Indonesia. It involved, among other things, a program of public exposure of the concept of anti-corruption and of the statute that had been drafted to implement such a concept.

The public exposure program involved public officials from various areas of Indonesia, along with officials from Jakarta and myself. We traveled to various regional centers throughout the country and discussed both the general concept of the anti-corruption agency being set up and the specifics of the statute as drafted. The meetings were attended by local government officials, by representatives of nongovernment organizations, and in some instances by invited members of the public. All were well attended. The questions posed by the attendees were often searching, indicating a keen interest in and appreciation of the issues involved. The topics debated varied according to the geographic area.

There was clear consensus that an organization dedicated to eradicating corruption was desirable, but views about its form and its prospects of success differed. The meeting participants recognized that political will was essential for its success, as were the caliber and reputations of those chosen to head the organization. They also understood that the task confronting the proposed organization was extremely challenging. Resistance was apparent in some areas from different sections of the public sector, principally from some police officers. The need for the organization to have a regional presence was recognized at the regional level as well as among central government officials.

Although the project was originally directed solely toward creating a dedicated anti-corruption agency in Indonesia, it was expanded as a result of the obvious enthusiasm and clear dedication to the success of the project on the part of then Attorney-General Minister Lopa (who has since died suddenly). At his request a second statute was drafted with the objective of expanding the definition of corruption as currently understood under Indonesian law and to facilitate proof of corruption in the Indonesian courts.

Before the Indonesian parliament could give final consideration to the draft statutes the government changed. President Megawati Soekarnoputri, the new president, indicated her support for setting up a dedicated anti-corruption agency in Indonesia and for the concept embodied in the legislation.

Legislation setting up a dedicated anti-corruption agency has now been enacted. The proposed legislation for expanding the definition of corruption under Indonesian law and facilitating its proof in the courts is still pending. There is some urgency to do this, because legislation currently limits the conditions under which bribery is a crime, making it difficult to secure convictions for the payment of bribes.

PAPUA NEW GUINEA

Work is continuing in Papua New Guinea to strengthen the powers and improve the performance of the Ombudsman Commission in relation to corruption. This initiative is being assisted by aid from Australia and involves, among other things, an officer who was the director of corruption prevention and education at the Independent Commission Against Corruption in New South Wales. The indications are that the project has produced good results to date.

INTERPOL

The IGEC, of which I am chairman, recommended to Interpol's General Assembly that minimum global standards in relation to the police forces and services of member nations should be produced and promulgated. At the General Assembly's 68th session, held in Seoul, Korea, in November 1999, it adopted the Seoul Declaration supporting minimum standards of ethical behavior and conduct in law enforcement agencies. The General Assembly expressly committed itself to underwriting the IGEC's anti-corruption initiatives, and at its 69th Session, held in Rhodes, Greece, in October-November 2000, mandated the IGEC to prepare a draft of such global standards for submission to the 70th session of the General Assembly, held in Budapest in September 2001.

In implementing the resolutions of the General Assembly, the IGEC determined that it should first conduct a short integrity survey of the police forces and services of member states. This was done, and the results are now being assessed. Concurrently global standards were prepared and recommended for consideration by the 70th Session of the General Assembly. At that session, the work of the IGEC was commended, and the standards as recommended were referred for comment by the member nations. The draft standards, along with appropriate amendments that may emerge from the comments of member states, will be discussed and adopted at the General Assembly's 71st session, to be held in 2002.

The concepts underlying the global standards, and which have been accepted by the General Assembly, are as follows:

- The recognition that corruption undermines the effectiveness and efficiency of law enforcement
- The belief that corruption can be prevented and eradicated
- The need for police forces and services to accept responsibility for detecting and holding accountable those in their ranks who are corrupt
- The awareness that political will and forceful action at the national level, assisted by international recognition of the problem and support at this level, are essential for the fight against corruption to succeed.

The draft global standards were given even wider exposure at the 10th International Anti-Corruption Conference held in Prague in October 2001, when they were presented to the law enforcement officers in attendance from many countries. The standards are also likely to be presented to and discussed at Interpol's regional meeting to be held in the Asia-Pacific region in the near future.

When adopted, the global standards should assist the wider efforts to combat corruption, especially in the public sectors of the region, and may provide an impetus for creating a set of standards for this sector.

NEPAL

An ADB-funded initiative in Nepal involves a number of Australians. The project is intended to help Nepal overcome certain hurdles that stand in the way of major loans to the country from international funding agencies. One component of the project is designed to improve levels of integrity and efficiency in the civil service and to help eradicate corruption. To date, an overall anti-corruption strategy has been formulated in conjunction with the government of Nepal and a number of local nongovernment organizations. In addition, a corporate plan has been prepared for the Nepalese Commission for the Investigation of the Abuse of Authority.

CONCLUSION

The support of the Australian government for these projects indicates heightened awareness about the problem of corruption in the public sector and in the region and growing concern on the part of governments in these different countries to put in place structures and programs to deal with the problem. The increasing concern about the dangers of corruption among the ADB's developing member countries and the need for urgent action needs to be matched by a similar sense of urgency in Australia and other donor countries and in international agencies. In the final analysis, the political will to empower and support those whose task it is to discover, investigate, reveal, and punish corruption in the public sector will be the major determinant of success. Support from this conference could assist in that regard.

B. Disclosure of Information

II. Disclosure of Information

Chapter 4

The Powerlessness of the Media in Pakistan

■ Zohra Yusuf

As Pakistan does not have any disclosure or freedom of information laws, this chapter focuses on the role of the media in exposing corruption. It also looks at the state of media freedom in Pakistan in the context of how effectively the media have played their role and concludes with some recommendations.

HISTORY OF COVER-UPS

To put the culture of secrecy that has been the norm in Pakistan in a historical perspective, we need to return to the time of Pakistan's independence. While many countries have been born out of bloody freedom struggles, India and Pakistan, created as a result of the division of the subcontinent in 1947, witnessed an unprecedented bloodbath following the announcement of their independence. Both countries had to cope with history's largest movement of refugees, and in addition, the seeds of suspicion and antagonism were sown with the unresolved status of Kashmir. Pakistan also felt vulnerable because of its separation by 1,000 miles of Indian territory from the former East Pakistan, now Bangladesh.

Pakistan's rulers believed that keeping the press under control and denying access to information was one of the ways to defend the country and cover up its weaknesses. However, corruption and cover-ups are inextricably linked. The mass migrations of the late 1940s led to windfalls for many bureaucrats in relation to properties left behind by Hindus. The exploitation of migrants' property for massive personal gain was the first instance of widespread corruption in Pakistan. The press, perhaps in the belief that exposing corruption in the newly independent state would be unpatriotic, exercised self-censorship and refrained from revealing what was going on. Moreover, bureaucrats trained in colonial ways had already introduced the system of "press advice," whereby formally, in writing, or informally, over the phone, editors were asked not to publish certain news items or opinions.

Control of the press and of the flow of information ensured that the web of corruption grew unchecked. The only exposures of government corruption became the official white papers issued by each successive government about the government it had overthrown. Such attempts at exposure not only lacked credibility, but created an environment whereby all officially disclosed cases of corruption were suspect. This is one of the reasons why the electorate has brought back into power governments dismissed because of charges of corruption.

RESTRICTIVE LAWS

The Byzantine workings of the bureaucratic mind in Pakistan (and of the prepartition colonial government) are revealed by the presence of 56 statutes, rules, and regulations dealing with the print media alone. In addition, about a dozen control mechanisms pertain to the audiovisual electronic media.

The mass media are also subject to other laws and to various sections of the 1860 Pakistan Penal Code as amended from time to time. Section 499, for example, relates specifically to defamation. The military government of General Ziaul Haq attempted to amend this section so as to make the publication of all negative stories about public officials, even if true, a punishable offense. In addition, the all-encompassing Official Secrets Act of 1923 classifies various documents so they cannot be revealed. The contempt of court law also restricts reporting about corrupt practices within the judiciary.

ABSENCE OF FREEDOM OF INFORMATION

Thus a vast array of laws controls the flow of information in Pakistan, which has yet to introduce a freedom of information act. Surprisingly, it is Pakistan's interim governments that have initiated, albeit in a limited way, the process of ensuring greater freedom of information. In September 1988, following the death of General Ziaul Haq in a plane crash, the caretaker government amended Pakistan's notorious 1963 Press and Publications Ordinance to ease the process of acquiring a declaration for a publication (previously publishers had had to wait for approval from a district magistrate to commence publication). Similarly, the interim government that followed the ouster of Benazir Bhutto's government promulgated the 1997 Freedom of Information Ordinance. This was—and remains—the first and only effort to make official records accessible to the public, although it also added certain restrictions, such as allowing the government to categorize banking company records, documents of a personal nature, and any other documents it chose as classified. An appeal, however, could be made to the federal ombudsman. The other ordinance promulgated during the same period was the Electronic Media Regulatory Authority, which would have allowed electronic media to broadcast news bulletins other than those produced by the state-owned Pakistan Television and Pakistan Broadcasting Corporation. The government of Nawaz Sharif, which came into power following the general elections in 1997, allowed both these ordinances to lapse.

EXPOSÉS FOLLOWING THE RESTORATION OF DEMOCRACY

Ever since the press gained a relative degree of freedom in the mid-1980s following General Ziaul Haq's death in 1988, exposés and stories about corruption have frequently hit the headlines of the national newspapers. The press's new-found freedom coincided with the return to democracy, with the result that democratically elected governments found themselves facing journalists keen to engage in investigative reporting. Regrettably, the newly elected government that came into power after a long struggle against the military establishment felt the need to reward its supporters and party workers. Worse still, its leaders decided to reward themselves too, and somewhat lavishly.

While Pakistani journalists had achieved mastery in writing between the lines under restrictions placed on them by successive military governments, they had only begun to flex the muscles of freedom when general elections brought the government of Benazir Bhutto into power in 1988. Before this time, even under military rule, several journalists had showed exemplary courage in exposing the corruption of certain members of the ruling junta, with the foremost instance being the reporting of the involvement of the military governor of the Frontier province in the heroin trade. Many journalists suffered as a result of the risks they took in exposing corruption among the country's most powerful people. Many were picked up and held incommunicado, were threatened, and were sometimes assaulted by unidentified men.

The civilian government gave the press not only the freedom it sought, but also the opportunity to break sensational news on corrupt practices. The latter, of course, was inadvertent. Several factors accounted for this sudden upsurge in reporting about corruption that went right up to the Prime Minister's Office. To begin with Benazir Bhutto and her husband demonstrated a certain degree of brazenness in their practice of corruption. When the president dismissed her based on charges of corruption and the misuse of power, newspaper reports formed the bulk of the evidence, and were even accepted by the superior courts that upheld the dismissal. This became a pattern. The two major parties ruled alternately until each was dismissed on charges of corruption under a controversial constitutional provision.

The source of information about corruption came primarily from press reports. Nevertheless, none of the cases resulted in conviction except for that against Benazir Bhutto, and that too was set aside by the Supreme Court following revelations that one of the judges who had heard her case had a conflict of interest. This reveals that the prosecution has failed to substantially prove the charges of corruption. Thus democratically elected governments have seen their terms of office end abruptly on the basis of disclosures in the press. On the one hand, investigative reporters in Pakistan have bemoaned the fact that their disclosures have been ineffective, and on the other hand have regretted their role in the bringing down of elected governments.

ROLE OF THE MILITARY AND OF INTELLIGENCE AGENCIES

Even today which of the disclosures appearing in the press were true and which were planted by one of Pakistan's intelligence agencies is unclear. Since its inception, Pakistan has been largely under the control of the military-bureaucracy combine. Suppressing information is an obsession the bureaucracy inherited from its colonial masters. Meanwhile the military has deemed it beneath its dignity to share information with the civilian population. Such issues as defense spending, details of military contracts, and so on are not debated in Parliament even when there is one.

The military and intelligence agencies have also played a dangerous part in corrupting the political and democratic process without being held accountable. In the 1988 general elections the then army chief (according to his own statement, given voluntarily) used Pakistan's most powerful intelligence agency, Inter-Services Intelligence, to distribute funds among political parties opposing the Pakistan People's Party. The objective was achieved: the creation of a right-wing coalition that ensured that Bhutto's party would not have a clear majority in Parliament and would consequently remain at the mercy of the military, unable to liberalize Pakistani society.

To some extent the military-bureaucracy combine has also been responsible for corruption among journalists. In the highly secretive environment of the military establishment, when a former chief of the Navy is exposed for corrupt practices in the purchase of submarines, the discerning reader knows that the exposé has in some way been facilitated. Journalists can also be used by vested interests in their differences with each other. .An example is the sensational story that broke during Benazir Bhutto's first tenure as prime minister. According to press reports her husband, Asif Zardari, had a bomb tied to an expatriate Pakistani businessman and forced him to withdraw all his money from a bank and hand it over to a crony of Zardari. Years later it became clear that the story was totally fabricated and planted. Successive civilian governments have also made the bribing of journalists a part of their media policy. Known as *lifafa* (envelope) journalism, reporters and editors have been paid to plant stories against political opponents.

Nevertheless, journalists as a whole have fought valiantly for the freedom of expression. Some have lost their jobs, and others even their lives, in attempts to expose corruption. While civilian governments and politicians have been easier targets, when information has become available journalist have not spared the military.

The July 2001 issue of *Herald,* a Karachi news magazine, carried a story about the auditor-general's report on corruption in the armed forces. As written in the *Herald:* "According to inquiries made by the AGP's office, the armed forces have caused the national exchequer a staggering loss of 20 billion rupees between 1987 and 1998 under the head of defense purchases alone. This does not include the millions of dollars paid out in commissions and kickbacks, Mansoorul Haq's Agosta-90B deal being a case in point."

CURBING CORRUPTION

Various governments have loudly proclaimed their efforts to combat corruption. In most cases, these efforts have been exercises in victimizing their political opponents or are generally perceived as such. In more recent years, the National Accountability Bureau of the military government has replaced the Accountability Cell of former Prime Minister Nawaz Sharif. The bureau (its acronym, NAB, always raises eyebrows) has itself not been forthcoming with information. It rarely explains the basis for releasing certain individuals arrested on corruption charges in a satisfactory way. Even today, the press carries speculative stories about the deal between the military government, the Sharifs, and the Saudis that resulted in the sudden exile of the entire family of the former prime minister.

NEW INITIATIVES

The present government is, reportedly, working on the framework for a freedom of information act to ensure greater transparency in the public interest. It is also believed that the contempt of court law will be amended to bring the judiciary within the ambit of public scrutiny. The proposed draft ordinance needs to be closely monitored so that it does not contain all the exclusions present in the previous lapsed ordinance.

MODEL FREEDOM OF INFORMATION LAW

Below are some of the recommendations arrived at by a group of representatives of international nongovernment organizations that met in Colombo in July 2001. The participants came up with the following set of recommendations as a guide to adopting information legislation:

- Establish a presumption in favor of disclosure, which is subject only to narrow and clearly drawn exceptions that include a harm test and a public interest override.
- Provide for an independent appeals mechanism for any refusals to disclose information that operates in a timely and low-cost fashion, and that has full powers to assess claims, including by viewing records, and to order disclosure.
- Ensure the existence of a body responsible for monitoring and promoting effective implementation of the law.
- Establish mechanisms for tackling the culture of secrecy, including through training.
- Require public bodies to publish and disseminate widely documents of significant public interest, subject only to reasonable limits based on resources and capacity.
- Impose the same obligations on private bodies that undertake public functions as on public bodies.
- Provide penalties for willful obstruction of access to information.
- Provide protection against legal, administrative, or employment-related sanctions for whistle-blowers and those who release information about wrongdoing or about serious threats to health and environmental safety, as long as they acted in good faith and in the reasonable belief that the information was substantially true and disclosed evidence of wrongdoing.
- Establish a right to receive information from private bodies where this information is needed to exercise or protect a right.

- Impose an obligation on private bodies to publish information in the general public interest, including where those bodies undertake activities posing a risk of harm to public health or safety or to the environment, or where this is necessary to enable consumers to make informed choices.

To be effective in checking corruption any freedom of information act will depend on an aware citizenry as well as on the opening up of the electronic media. The re-election of corrupt leaders stems from the choices made by a largely illiterate and ill-informed electorate. However, even illiterate citizens are suspicious of the government-controlled electronic news media and rarely believe the official disclosures of corruption. Exposure of corruption in the independent print media reaches an extremely small proportion of Pakistan's citizens, that is, the educated, who also happen to be the most apathetic when it comes to political participation.

In recent years Pakistan has improved its position on Transparency International's list of corrupt countries. Disclosure laws are essential to ensure that no backsliding occurs, and freedom of information laws need to be supported by a freer media and greater support from civil society.

Since the initial writing of this chapter, the government has introduced a new electronic media regulatory authority to facilitate the setting up of radio and television channels in the private sector. These would be allowed to broadcast independent current affairs programs and news.

The government is also discussing with representatives of the press, the drafts of a proposed freedom of information act, as well as a controversial defamation law.

Chapter 5

Establishing Mechanisms to Ensure Free Public Access to Information—Practices and Problems

■ **Akira Yamada**

I n Japan, the system for disclosure of administrative information started at the local government level. After Kanagawa prefecture introduced an information disclosure ordinance in 1982, many prefectures enacted their own information disclosure ordinances during the 1980s and early 1990s. The national Law on Information Disclosure was finally passed in 1999 and became law in April 2001. While the law's content is similar to that of equivalent laws in other industrial countries, for a number of reasons Japan adopted such a law later than many other nations.

To begin with, in a number of industrial countries opposition parties demanded that governments pass an information disclosure law, and when those opposition parties came into office, they were obliged to set up an information disclosure system whether or not they still wanted to. Thus in some cases a change of administration resulted in an information disclosure system. In Japan, the Liberal Democratic Party held on to power from the 1950s until 1993, when the opposition took over, which was around the same time that the movement for passage of an information disclosure law became serious.

The underlying philosophy of the current law on information disclosure is the government's accountability. The actual wording in the law is *setsumei sekinin*, which literally means "responsibility of explanation." Japanese does not have an exact equivalent of the word "accountability," and few Japanese understood this word in the 1980s. This suggests that the actual concept of accountability did not exist in the administration.

Until the mid-1980s, while the Japanese had little trust in politics or politicians, they generally appreciated the work of members of the civil service and trusted them. Civil service bureaucrats themselves believed that they were doing good job and felt no need to explain the detailed workings of the administration to the public. However, following a number of scandals in the administration in the mid-1980s and the deteriorating economic situation in the mid-1990s, people began to lose their faith in the bureaucracy. They became more forceful in their opinions that the government should provide more explanation about its policies and administrative measures and should disclose more information so as to engender open discussion on public policies. Their demands included the passage of an information disclosure law.

The Law on Information Disclosure contains a review clause whereby after four years it will be reexamined. As the law as only been in effect for less than a year, it is currently too early to assess its impact; however, some problems have already become apparent. The most serious problem is the shortage of resources, especially human resources, to carry out the work involved in information disclosure. To do such work properly, officials should understand the law well, be able to identify documents requested and find them, and must follow stipulated internal procedures. If the disclosure is a partial one, the officials should know which parts of the documents requested should be blacked out.

All these procedures imply a huge work load. During the first six months about 26,000 requests for information disclosure were received. Some ministry departments received hundreds of requests at the same time. Thus civil servants could either neglect their routine work to comply with the time frame for information disclosure stipulated in the law or attempt to carry out some of their regular duties and risk contravening the law.

During the course of administrative reforms the number of civil servants has been decreasing every year. Only a few additional officials were added when the law came into effect, and most of these were assigned to work at windows where they deal directly with the public. In addition, interpretations of the law are still under way. Thus given the shortage of staff, the initial onslaught of requests for information, and a certain lack of clarity in relation to the law's intent, the system has been somewhat overwhelmed; however, once it becomes well established, such problems should diminish.

The views in this chapter are the author's own and do not represent either the official views of the Japanese government or of the Information Disclosure Review Board.

Another problem is the balance between protecting personal information and disclosing administrative information. According to the law, anyone may request the disclosure of administrative information and administrative bodies must decide on access based on the requester. If individuals want to obtain information about themselves, in many cases such requests will be denied based on the law's prohibition against disclosing personal information. The law should address this type of problem, but currently does not. In this connection a committee recently issued a report and a new law is expected to be enacted shortly that will enter into force by July 2003.

In addition to the disclosure of official government information the public also called for information disclosure by independent administrative institutions and public corporations. A new law to this end has been passed and will take effect in July 2002.

The introduction of an information disclosure system changes and is changing work processes in the administration, both at the national government level and at local government levels in ways that are both positive and negative. On the negative side, officials tend to avoid writing documents on delicate issues under consideration, because they are afraid of the disclosure of such documents. They may be ready in principle to explain and be accountable to the people for their work, but they know that in practice explaining the reasons for some of their decisions may be difficult and time-consuming. There are also problems with policy options that are considered and then discarded. In Japan the mass media tend to criticize officials for their opinions even when these are not incorporated in final policies. Thus officials may fear that any radical and innovative options they put forward for consideration—and that they themselves may view as fallacious in the light of subsequent debate—will be criticized as though they were firm recommendations. Thus a reluctance to commit matters to writing may be unfortunate, but it is understandable. On the positive side, public officials now have a greater sense of responsibility and keep the spirit of accountability in mind during the course of their work. They are now more interested in doing a good job from the public's point of view than from the point of view of administrative insiders.

Given an information disclosure mechanism, if public servants believe they are doing a good job, they can feel that the public trusts their work more than in the past, because citizens now have the ability to monitor their activities. While an information disclosure system cannot by itself eliminate corruption, it can create an environment in which engaging in corruption is more difficult.

Citizen groups have used information disclosure ordinances to check for the inappropriate use of public funds, and have achieved some concrete results. While there is plenty of room for improvement, information disclosure mechanisms at the local government level have played an important role in enhancing the transparency of local governments.

During the first eight months after the law came into effect, most of those requesting information were mass media journalists. Ordinary citizens do not request information disclosure often; however, to improve the public's perception of the administration, the government should attempt to make information public voluntarily without waiting for requests for information to be disclosed.

Remember above all that the system is new. Once it has become better understood by both civil servants and the public, I am confident that it will enhance the overall quality of life in Japan.

Chapter 6

Disclosure of Information by the Asian Development Bank

■ **Clay Wescott**

ADB staff are increasingly recognizing that the Bank should provide the greatest possible degree of transparency and accountability in its activities to ensure the success of its mission and to sustain public support, while bearing in mind important legal and practical constraints. These are competing needs that must be reconciled under a readily understandable and consistent policy.

DEVELOPING CURRENT POLICY AND PRACTICE

The ADB's policy on confidentiality and disclosure of information came into effect on 1 January 1995. Prior to that time, the Bank's policy had become relatively complex, inconsistent, and outdated. This had led to confusion on the part of the staff, which led to caution and defensiveness when they had to release information or documents. Moreover, the classification system did not reflect the trend within the ADB to encourage the dissemination of information as widely as possible.

The trend toward greater disclosure was also evident in other international finance institutions such as the World Bank, which shares both the same interests in disseminating information on its operations and activities and similar constraints and restrictions on such dissemination relating to the rights and interests of member countries, property owners, staff, and others. Starting in 1993, the World Bank has increasingly been making documents available to the public through public information centers, web sites, and other channels.

The ADB's disclosure policy (ADB 1996) benefited from the World Bank's experience. The advantages of a policy encouraging the fullest possible disclosure of operational information are readily apparent. Such advantages include the following:

- Encouraging debate and dialogue on the organization's policies and operations, which in turn results in an increased flow of information back to the ADB, thereby providing new and varied perspectives
- Helping to ensure effective local participation in decisionmaking, which leads to the "ownership" of decisions by involved participants, thereby improving project implementation and sustainability
- Broadening the understanding of the ADB's role among donor member countries, borrowing member countries, cofinanciers, nongovernment organizations, academic institutions, and the general public, thereby helping to ensure both financial and intellectual support for the ADB and its mission
- Facilitating coordination with others interested in the common goal of development of the region
- Recognizing that as a public institution the ADB is accountable to its shareholders and others that provide support to the institution and has a responsibility to provide them with the fullest possible information.

Notwithstanding these advantages, the ADB must also take into account legal and practical constraints relating to the disclosure of information in order to protect the ADB's interests and the legitimate interests of those who deal with the ADB, and to sustain cooperative relationships with its various member countries. These constraints, which should be balanced against the ADB's presumption in favor of disclosure, include the following:

- Information provided to the ADB on a confidential basis cannot be released without the prior consent or approval of the party providing such information. In some cases, such confidentiality relates to legal requirements in the jurisdiction of the party providing the information, or is governed by an agreement or understanding between the ADB and the party providing the information. In other cases maintaining confidentiality is simply a good business practice to ensure the continuous flow of information from the provider, which may be a government, a cofinancier, or a private party.
- Documentation or proprietary information may be the legal property of other parties, and therefore the ADB cannot release it without the permission of such owners.
- To encourage frank dialogue and the free flow of ideas internally, protecting the integrity of the ADB's deliberative processes is essential. Thus internal documents prepared by staff or management, including initial negotiating positions and committee deliberations, must be protected. For example, the Board's proceedings are confidential, and such proceedings have been interpreted to include the internal

processing of documents. The confidentiality that protects these decisionmaking processes ensures that all participants can candidly express their views without self-imposed limitations in anticipation of an external audience.

- The ADB has a working relationship with its borrowing members, often sharing privileged information, particularly with respect to policy dialogue on critical matters. Just as internal information must flow on a free and confidential basis to ensure frank and candid discussions, so borrowing members and the ADB must be able to undertake free and candid discussions on the basis of reciprocal respect for the confidential character of information.

- In private sector operations the ADB must protect the legitimate business interests and proprietary information of private sector clients to preserve its ability to carry on such activities.

- The ADB has a general obligation to establish and maintain safeguards with respect to the personal privacy of its staff and to protect the confidentiality of their personal information.

One additional constraint relates to the cost of information disclosure. While the ADB's policies should encourage the greatest possible disclosure of information, in the light of limited financial resources, the cost to the ADB of disseminating information and the issue of cost recovery, if appropriate, must be considered. To the extent feasible, ADB staff will provide summaries of or "information pieces" concerning ADB documents so as to facilitate the disclosure of information and minimize the cost to the public and the ADB of providing such information.

IMPLEMENTING THE POLICY

The policy provides new procedures for classifying documents and makes them more readily available.

How Are Documents Classified?

Under its new policy the ADB adopted a streamlined system with three document classifications: "confidential," "for official use only," and "unclassified." Confidential documents are those that contain particularly sensitive information and are intended for limited internal use within the Bank, and whose release is likely to have a serious adverse effect on, or be prejudicial to, the interests of the Bank or its stakeholders. In addition, documents classified as confidential should relate to at least one of the following categories:

- Information or documentation obtained by the Bank from another party with the expectation, expressed or implied, that it will be kept in confidence
- Documents or proprietary information owned by others but held by the Bank in the expectation, expressed or implied, that it will be kept in confidence
- Information derived from the Bank's deliberative or decisionmaking process, such as internal staff memoranda and minutes and summaries of discussions at Board meetings, unless authorization has been given to disclose such information
- Information derived from similar decisionmaking processes involving open and candid exchanges of ideas between the Bank and any of its member countries, particularly with respect to policy dialogue
- Legal and other documents relating to specific private sector investments, including private sector investments by a government or governmental entity, unless the parties concerned have consented to disclosure
- Staff information of a personal nature, such as personnel records and medical files (except for disclosure to the individual staff member concerned).

A confidential document is made available only to Bank staff with a demonstrated need to know the information contained in the document. In general, documents marked confidential by a government will be declassified and released only with the government's consent.

Documents classified for official use only are those determined to contain sensitive information for the internal use of the Bank, the release of which could jeopardize its activities or relationships with stakeholders, but which do not include confidential information. Information or documents classified as for official use only are normally declassified within five years of the date of classification. To the extent possible, the Bank will not permit information relevant to a significant allegation of criminal behavior or unethical conduct, including conflict of interest, to remain classified as confidential or for official use only.

This classification system is also be applicable to all electronically-based and computer-generated information, as well as photographic and graphic materials.

When documents previously classified as confidential or for official use only are released to the public, sensitive information not appropriate for disclosure is deleted from the documents when necessary pursuant to management instructions. In other cases the ADB may attach a statement to the document being released indicating that the ADB does not accept responsibility for the views expressed by the document's authors.

What Is Disclosed and When?

Under the new policy, documents to be disclosed include those with basic information about the ADB, such as its annual report, and many others, including the following:

- Project or program profiles, which make project information available to interested parties while a project is still under preparation
- Report and recommendation of the president for a project or program loan
- Technical assistance reports
- Country economic reviews
- Country operation strategy studies
- Country strategy and program, previously referred to as the country assistance plan, which includes performance assessments and project pipelines for developing member countries
- Postevaluation reports
- Sector policy papers
- Environment-related documents, including summary environmental impact assessments, environmental impact assessments, initial environmental examinations, and summary environmental examinations
- Other technical information, such as additional information or technical documents relating to a public sector project, program, or technical assistance under preparation or implementation, which may be declassified in part or in full after consultation with the government, borrower, or recipient concerned.

For example, the ADB now publishes detailed project profiles that describe the main elements of a proposed project or program, including its environmental aspects; social information, including information about resettlement and indigenous peoples; and dates for public consultations if arranged by the proposed borrower or sponsor (ADB 2002). The purpose of the profiles is to provide as much information as possible to the public during the earliest stages of project preparation to ensure adequate debate, dialogue, and participation by the parties concerned, including affected populations, at the formative stages of a project. After approval, copies of the relevant project document are declassified, and can be obtained by the general public. Feasibility studies arising from technical assistance reports can also be released except to the extent classified by the government concerned. Similarly, country strategy papers and other analytical papers are normally released following approval.

Similarly, the ADB adopts a presumption in favor of disclosure for its private sector operations where disclosure would not materially harm the business and competitive interests of ADB clients. Any disclosure by the ADB regarding the business plans and objectives of a private sector client is only made with the client's consent.

Where Can You Find and Order Documents?

Under the disclosure policy, information is available through printed publications, web sites (the main portal is http://www.adb.org), news releases, advertisements, and depository libraries. Public information centers are also available at ADB headquarters in Manila, in resident missions, and in representative offices. Any department or office receiving a request for information or documents relays such a request within three working days to the Information Office, which will arrange for a review of the request by the relevant ADB office and, where appropriate, by the government concerned. The relevant ADB office will give particular regard to the classification of the information or documents and provide a response to the request, either by providing such information or indicating the reasons such information cannot be provided, within 22 working days of the ADB's receipt of the request.

Disclosure of documents is free, but the ADB charges $10 for each hard copy provided to help defray costs with two exceptions: environment documents are provided free of charge, and documents on a particular country are free of charge to requesters from that country. Documents are sent by courier. The most recent publications are also available for free on http://www.adb.org. Documents can be requested by email from adbpub@adb.org; by mail from ADB Publications Unit, P.O. Box 789, 0980 Manila, Philippines; or by fax from 632-636-2648.

NEXT STEPS

In 2001 the World Bank revised its disclosure policy once again to provide for the release of more documents, including the chairman's summaries of key Board discussions, in a more timely manner, with improved access through World Bank country offices.

The ADB believes that its disclosure policy meets most current needs. Minor problems relating to implementation and outreach could be resolved by educating requesters and staff on who does what and what is disclosed. Many ADB departments are involved, which makes for some coordination problems. In some cases, requesters ask several staff for the same information, which means that different staff are all working on the same request. To address these minor problems, the ADB is preparing a list of all categories of documents to be disclosed, which will be made into a matrix for staff and will list document type, status (disclosed/not disclosed), how to request, how to respond to external requests, how to request document disclosure, and who to contact in case of problems. With training for staff and outreach for external requesters, the hope is that disclosure practices at the ADB will continue to improve.

REFERENCES

ADB (Asian Development Bank). 1996. Policy on Confidentiality and Disclosure of Information: A Guidebook. Manila.

_____. 2002. *ADB Business Opportunities* (monthly). (On-line). Available: http://www.adb.org/Business/Opportunities/default.asp.

C. Integrity in Politics

Chapter 7

Enforcing Accountability by and the Transparency of Political Parties

■ **Lim Guan Eng**

Integrity is a rare commodity, especially in politics. In an environment of systemic nonintegrity, politicians who aspire to live up to high standards of accountability often do not last. When the private and public sectors are closely intertwined, without the right links to the business world a political career is invariably an uncertain undertaking. Conversely, successfully managing a private enterprise is a difficult task without the right political connections. Most political parties have their own investment arms that monopolize the print and electronic media, the banking and financial sectors, and some industrial sectors. In such a system corruption and bribery find fertile soil.

CAPTIVE CORRUPTION

For a number of well-placed individuals, corruption can be beneficial; however, given the extensive harm that it does to a country's economy, the argument that corruption can contribute to its economic development by serving as grease money to speed up certain procedures can hardly be considered correct. Similarly, huge capital expenditure by governments is often said to be an indispensable engine of economic growth, but if corruption is present the reverse is more likely to be the case. According to Tanzi and Davoodi (1998), corruption combined with such large public investments is likely to reduce growth by

- Increasing total public investment while reducing its productivity
- Increasing public investment that is not adequately supported by nonwage expenditures on operations and maintenance
- Reducing the quality of existing infrastructure
- Decreasing the government revenues needed to finance productive spending.

Capital expenditure by governments presents another source of fertile ground for corruption. The total amount of current government expenditure determines the level of government revenues needed, while capital spending is the main determinant of economic growth. This risks to provide a blank check for unnecessary government borrowing to cover fiscal deficits in order to justify extensive capital expenditure and other forms of mismanagement of government revenue. With regard to public spending, while politicians' discretion is limited given that most current spending by governments reflects previous commitments, such as pension and interest payments, public debt repayments, salaries, and subsidies, the situation is different in the context of new capital projects, where their discretion is large, thereby opening up vast opportunities for corruption. Thus major public investments in an environment where corruption is endemic carry the risk of bringing about more economic harm than benefit to a country.

ACCOUNTING FOR ASSETS AND INTEREST

To combat systemic corruption, relying on politicians with personal integrity is not the complete answer. Transparency and accountability must be institutionalized, with rules in place that pertain to full disclosure, freedom of information, public declaration of personal assets, and open invitation to public scrutiny.

If government leaders are not required to declare their assets publicly, which is the situation in Malaysia and elsewhere in the region, they and their families can accumulate wealth that might not always be justified. In addition to depriving society of resources, and thereby hindering necessary public investments to reduce poverty and foster economic growth, this contributes to the decline of public trust in government. To counter this problem governments need to implement rules and regulations governing conflicts of interest and requiring the disclosure of personal assets and liabilities by politicians and civil servants.

EMPOWERING CIVIL SOCIETY

In this context, it is worrying that the particularly high public perception of the level of corruption in Malaysia, as reflected in Transparency International's corruption perception index and other similar indexes, is combined with a tendency among the public to be inured to, passive about, and even tolerant of perceived corrupt practices. The loss of significant public funds as a consequence of corruption is certainly a serious problem, but much more troubling is if such wrongdoing is not sanctioned. This leads to a public that can only be shocked by scandals of particularly striking moral concern, such as the recent finding that law students, supposedly the future defenders of law and justice, are willing to pay large amounts of money for leaked examination papers.

Therefore awareness raising and capacity building in civil society to stimulate public opposition against corruption and gain civil society's support for the fight against corruption are crucial for bringing about change. The effectiveness of such public support was demonstrated in a case concerning improper management of the budget of the government of the Malaysian state of Malacca. Malacca's annual budget deficit increased by almost 400 percent, from RM50 million in 2000 to RM 242 million in 2001, or around RM350 for each of Malacca's 600,000 residents. This sudden increase was due to a publics works and capital expenditure program, especially the construction of a RM500 million dam. While the need for additional water in Malacca was widely acknowledged, the construction of a large dam in a relatively small state was seen as a potential threat to the environment, the livelihood of residents, and the long-term sustainability of the rain forests, and provoked speculation that the dam project might be an attempt to justify a potentially illicit capital expenditure and to hide it behind the need for water.

Investigations into this case revealed that at a previous Malacca State Assembly meeting in 1999 the construction costs had been evaluated at RM161 million, as opposed to the RM500 million stated later. This resulted in a public campaign demanding full transparency and accountability in relation to this project, as well as an explanation of the RM339 million difference. The state government could not explain this increase in costs by, for instance, pointing to additional specifications to the dam, and consequently decided to call for a public tender.

An examination of 16 volumes of tender documents did indeed reveal some differences in specifications. The dam's height had increased by 5 percent and the crest length had increased by 44 percent, but these changes were not significant enough to justify such a large cost increase. Worse still, the dam's production capacity under the new tender had decreased by 400 percent. At the end of the investigation the state government had to give in to intense public pressure and award the tender for the dam at a cost of RM118 million. The resulting savings of RM382 million could immediately be used to maintain water rates at the same level for the following five years. Thus at a time when almost every state in Malaysia was increasing water rates, the Malacca state government was in a position where it could ensure that its citizens had access to water resources at adequate rates.

This was one of the few instances where a public campaign succeeded in curbing corrupt practices. It is also an example of how an empowered and educated civil society and a healthy democracy are probably the most effective tools against corruption. However, successfully mobilizing society requires sufficient resources, both in terms of finances and in terms of human capital.

ENFORCING ANTI-CORRUPTION LAWS

An independent judicial system based on the rule of law is another prerequisite for an effective fight against corruption. Malaysia's anti-corruption laws are governed by the 1997 Anti-Corruption Act, an extensive piece of legislation, and effected by the Anti-Corruption Agency. However, proper implementation and enforcement of these laws face challenges because of a lack of politicians with integrity and strong political will, and because of political interference in the agency's investigations. Only a few high-level political leaders have been prosecuted under these laws, and usually when they have been shorn of political support by those in power.

Strict enforcement of the act is more often punished than praised, as demonstrated by the investigation against a former Malaysian deputy prime minister. Instead of being praised for bringing a senior government civil servant to justice for an unexplained RM100,000 in cash found during a raid of his office, the head of the Anti-Corruption Agency was forced to abandon the case on the grounds that the raid had been conducted without the prime minister's permission. The senior civil servant accused in this case was subsequently appointed as head of Malaysia's central bank.

In the absence of political will and of politicians with integrity, the most rigorous laws become ineffective. Corruption exists everywhere and can never be completely eliminated, but effective enforcement of proper anti-corruption laws can help reduce it. Malaysia's opposition parties should do their part by dealing with this problem, starting within their own ranks. While the magnitude of the problem within opposition parties is less significant, their credibility is at stake if they do not uphold the underlying principles and values of a stand against corruption and apply these principles to themselves first.

CONCLUSION

No one dares to dispute the negative consequences of corruption, but some still tend to condone it as a necessary evil of economic development.

Many governments in the region were once examples of this kind of thinking; however, the fallacy of this argument was exposed following the 1997 Asian financial crisis, which demonstrated how corruption had short-changed the country. The example of Singapore was proof of the argument that a clean government is best positioned to handle an economic crisis.

How can integrity in politics be restored when corrupt practices are rampant? The primary and most important prerequisite for such undertaking is political will. Battling corruption is a painful task for many governments, but a necessary one, and a famous Chinese proverb says: "Better a short pain than a long pain." But how many are willing to endure even a short pain, especially when no rewards are in sight? When eliminating corruption means risking their own demise, few governments can muster the political will necessary for such an undertaking. Therefore to foster the necessary political will, society at large and top leaders have to recognize and publicly acclaim the benefits for all of a corruption-free society, and those that are actively engaged in taking action against corruption need to be rewarded for their courageous undertaking.

Equally important is a democratic culture based on the rule of law that permits open public scrutiny and effective political opposition. While a country may not be able to eradicate corruption completely, it should have sufficient institutional mechanisms to punish corrupt behavior and strong public opinion so that those who engage in corruption genuinely fear sanctions, and are deterred from continuing their wrongdoing. Another old Chinese proverb says: "If you are thinking a year ahead, sow a seed. If you are thinking 10 years ahead, plant a tree. If you are thinking 100 years ahead, educate the people." The most effective remedy is to educate the young so that they grow up abhorring corrupt practices and are given the knowledge necessary to build a clean and trustworthy society, free of corruption, to the benefit of all.

REFERENCES

Tanzi, Vito, and Hamid Davoodi. 1998. *Roads to Nowhere: How Corruption in Public Investment Hurts Growth.* International Monetary Fund, Washington, D.C.

Chapter 8

Bribery and Political Parties: The OECD Convention

■ **Enery Quinones**

Thisthis chapter focuses on bribery transactions that are criminalized under the Convention on Combating Bribery of Foreign Public Officials in International Business Transactions. The convention has now been ratified by 34 countries: 29 OECD countries and 5 nonmember countries. The convention targets the practice of paying bribes to foreign public officials to obtain or retain international business.

Some are concerned that as the effectiveness of the convention increases, the likelihood of people finding ways to circumvent it will also increase. Their criticism is that by not expressly prohibiting bribery of foreign political parties or candidates for public office, payments that might have been made to foreign officials will be diverted to political parties and candidates in an attempt to gain favorable influence over government decisions.

DEFINITION OF FOREIGN PUBLIC OFFICIAL

It is true that the convention does not define political parties or party officers as people covered by the definition of foreign public official. This problem was discussed at length during the negotiations on the convention; however, because of divergent views among the different countries, consensus could not be reached. Those in favor of including political parties and party officers argued that bribing political parties and party officials was no less a breach of public trust than bribing public officials, and that the harmful consequences were no less pernicious. Those opposed to this view believed that their legal systems could not endorse the assimilation of these categories of people in the definition of foreign public official. In addition, they feared that because of the difficulty of defining a political party and a party officer, the autonomous definition of public official (one that does not rely on the definition of public official in a third country) in the convention would be endangered.

BRIBERY OF FOREIGN POLITICAL PARTIES

Even though the definition does not explicitly cover political parties and party officials, the convention does cover certain bribery transactions involving these people, namely:

- The bribing of a political party officer who also happens to be a public official, for example, a member of parliament, might be viewed as falling within the definition of foreign public official covered by the convention.
- A party officer who acts as an intermediary between a briber and a public official would also be included under the convention, because it covers both indirect as well as direct bribery.
- A bribery transaction between a briber and a public official that benefited a political party and party officer would also be covered by the convention.

In some situations coverage of bribery transactions involving political parties and party officers under the convention would depend on the actual circumstances of the case, for example:

- If party officers operate in a one-party state they may exercise public authority, in which case they could be treated as public officials under the convention.
- If political parties or party officers are in collusion with bribers they might be considered as a party, or co-author, to the transaction.

Let us now consider situations where bribery transactions involving political parties, and party officials are not covered and the significance of such noncoverage. Assume that someone has bribed a foreign political party officer to obtain an act or a decision by the party or the party officer. As this normally does not involve a government act or decision and as no foreign public official is involved, this may be a crime under some countries' national laws, but is not a crime under the convention. Similarly, if a foreign political party or party officials receive a bribe for the party or the officials to use their influence to obtain an act or decision by the government, this would also not be covered by the convention, but again, could be a crime under some national laws.

The question here is whether this behavior should be criminalized, and if so, in what manner? The next section assumes that the problem is significant enough to warrant such action and examines possible approaches.

SOLUTIONS

Some countries have already gone beyond the requirements of the convention and their national laws prohibit such conduct. For example, the United States includes bribery of a political party or a party official as an offense under its Foreign Corrupt Practices Act, and this covers both situations described in the previous section. Three other countries that have ratified the convention have included in their implementing laws the offense of bribing a party or a party officer in order to favorably influence a government decision. Other countries may have other national laws, such as those governing trafficking in influence, that may also cover this behavior. The problem is that the lack of uniformity could hamper the provision of mutual legal assistance or extradition where these are conditional on dual criminality.

A more uniform, multilateral approach, might be achieved in different stages as follows:

- In the short term, monitoring of the strict enforcement of the convention is imperative, so that the provisions that would punish bribery transactions involving political parties are applied by all countries party to the convention. This monitoring function implies reviewing by the OECD Secretariat of implementation laws to ensure that they effectively transpose the obligations of the convention (phase 1 of monitoring) and, more important, checking that countries are investigating, and if necessary, prosecuting, alleged bribery cases that would be covered under the convention (phase 2 of monitoring).
- In the medium term, continued assessment of the scope of the problem is needed. The OECD has begun to gather information on bribery in relation to political parties, party officials, and candidates for political office as part of the exercise to determine the significance of the potential loophole in the convention (see http://www.oecd.org/daf/nocorruption for the questionnaire). Depending on the responses, the OECD will consider steps to ensure more adequate coverage.
- By 2004 the OECD should be in a position either to issue a clarification that leaves no doubt about the scope of coverage of the convention or, if justified, to modify or amend the convention.

Another possible solution might be to develop a global convention that covers bribery in the private sector as well. The rationale would be to eliminate the current differentiation so that bribery of public officials and of anyone in the private sector would be considered as offenses. Before taking such a step, a study of the impact of a private sector convention on the existing convention on combating public sector bribery would be necessary; however, some organizations like Transparency International are urging the OECD in this direction.

While striving to achieve a more comprehensive solution, we must not lose sight of our immediate objectives. We should be conscientious in applying the convention we already have. Effectively enforcing existing laws is the best way to maintain credibility and people's perceptions that we will succeed in reducing corrupt payments in international business transactions.

PART II

Preventive and Enforcement Measures for Fighting Bribery

D. Prevention: What Businesses Can Do —
   Corporate Governance and Compliance
   Schemes
E. The Role of the Judiciary: Improving the
   Investigation and Prosecution of Bribery

**D. Prevention: What Businesses Can Do —
Corporate Governance and Compliance
Schemes**

Chapter 9

Corporate Governance in India

■ **Omkar Goswami**

S ince the second half of the 19th century, most modern industries and services in India have been structured under the English common law framework of joint stock limited liability. Despite this long corporate history, the term "corporate governance" remained unknown until 1993. It came to the fore at that time because of a spate of corporate scandals that occurred during the first flush of economic liberalization.[1]

The first was a major securities scam that was uncovered in April 1992. This involved a large number of banks, and resulted in the stock market nose-diving for the first time since the advent of reforms in 1991.[2] The second was a sudden growth of cases where multinational companies started consolidating their ownership by issuing preferential equity allotments to their controlling group at steep discounts to their market price (for details see Goswami 1996, pp. 124-25). The third scandal involved disappearing companies during 1993-94. Between July 1993 and September 1994 the stock index shot up by 120 percent. During this boom, hundreds of obscure companies made public issues at large share premiums, buttressed by sales pitch by obscure investment banks and misleading prospectuses. The management of most of these companies siphoned off the funds, and a vast number of small investors were saddled with illiquid stocks of dud companies. This shattered investor confidence and resulted in the virtual destruction of the primary market for the next six years.

---

[1] Similarly, in the United States corporate governance came into prominence only after the second oil shock in 1979. In the United Kingdom corporate governance started to be discussed only in the late 1980s and early 1990s in response to the collapse of the Bank of Credit and Commerce International and malpractice by the Maxwell group.

[2] Refer to the Mehta cartel case in the early 1990s, which resulted in the Bombay stock exchange, Sensex, being pushed up by almost 150 percent between December 1991 and April 1992, followed by a crash before the next boom began. The crash, which destroyed a large number of small retail investors and brokers, resulted in general questioning of the ability of banking and capital market regulators to ensure transparency and safety.

These three episodes led to the prominence of the concept of corporate governance among the financial press, banks and financial institutions, mutual funds, shareholders, more enlightened business associations, regulatory agencies, and the government. Note that unlike in Southeast and East Asia, the corporate governance movement did not occur because of a national or regionwide macroeconomic and financial collapse. Indeed, the Asian crisis barely touched India.

Today, increasing numbers of listed companies have begun to realize the need for transparency and good governance to attract both foreign and domestic capital. A growing number of chief executive officers now recognizes that complex cross-holdings, opaque financial disclosures, rubber-stamp boards, and inadequate concern for minority shareholders is a recipe for being shut out of competitive capital markets. Thus almost nine years after the start of economic liberalization, the beginnings of desirable corporate governance practices can be discerned, and indicators suggests that the trend will intensify in the next few years.

HISTORICAL BACKGROUND

In many ways India was unlike other former colonies in Asia or Africa. At the time of independence in 1947, India was one of the poorest nations in the world with a per capita annual income of less than $30. Yet manufacturing accounted for almost a fifth of national product, and half of that was contributed by the modern factory sector, which included cotton, iron and steel, and jute mills; collieries; nascent engineering units and foundries; and cement, sugar, and paper factories.

From the 1870s the growth of this sector was structured along corporate lines through joint stock limited liability companies, most of which were floated in India and listed on local stock exchanges. The Bombay Stock Exchange (BSE) was established in 1875, and began trading three years before the Tokyo Stock Exchange. At the beginning of the 20th century India had four fully functioning stock exchanges in Bombay, Calcutta, Madras and Ahmedabad, with well-defined listing, trading, and settlement rules.

The vehicle for corporate growth was the managing agency, a closely held company or partnership that functioned like a holding company. Managing agencies would float companies, and their imprimatur sufficed to ensure massive oversubscription of shares. Given excess demand, most major companies could split their shareholdings into small enough allotments to ensure that nobody other than the managing agency had enough stock to ensure their presence on the board of directors. Thus dispersed ownership allowed managing agencies to retain corporate control with relatively low equity ownership, a trend that continued until some 10 to 15 years ago. Thus from the corporate governance point of view, the tendency for management in India to enjoy control rights that are disproportionately greater than residual cash flow rights goes back to the early years of the 20th century.

On the positive side, because much corporate growth in pre-independence India was financed through equity, by the 1950s urban investors had developed a sophisticated equity culture. Moreover, the banking sector was surprisingly well developed for a country as poor as India. Banks were privately owned, advanced working capital, maintained prudential lending and accounting norms, and were backed up by sound recovery laws and efficient processes.

As modern industrial growth was structured along corporate lines, it is not surprising that colonial India quickly put in place a substantive body of corporate law. For instance, the periodically amended 1956 Companies Act, which governs the legal and regulatory aspects of public and private limited companies, derives from earlier Indian companies acts. Similarly, most of today's legal jurisdiction for corporate matters and disputes predates independence, as does legislation aimed at prudent regulation of banks. The law that regulates stock exchanges and the transactions of securities was also passed in 1956.

Thus in 1947 India had a sizable corporate sector that accounted for at least 10 percent of gross domestic product; it had well functioning stock markets and a developed banking system; it had a substantial body of laws relating to the conduct of companies, banks, stock markets, trusts, and securities; and it had an equity culture among the urban populace. It was probably the former colonial country that was best equipped to practice good corporate governance, maximize long-term corporate interests, and protect stakeholder rights. However, it did not do so.

The first barrier to investment came with the 1951 Industries (Development and Regulation) Act, which required all existing and proposed industrial units to obtain licenses from the central government. The licensing regime led to widespread rent-seeking. Entrepreneurial families and business groups that had built their fortunes in textiles, coal, iron and steel, and jute now used licenses to secure monopolistic and oligopolistic privileges in new industries such as aluminum, paper, cement, and engineering. Over the years licensing became increasingly stringent and was accompanied by multiple procedures that required clearances from many ministries. For instance, a typical private manufacturing company needed government permission to establish a new plant, manufacture a new article, expand its capacity, change its location, import capital goods, and do many other things that fell under the rubric of normal corporate activity. This law was abolished in 1991.

A more serious barrier to entry occurred in 1956, when in a move toward socialism the Industrial Policy Resolution stipulated that the public sector would dominate the economy and specified those industries for which the state would exclusively or increasingly be responsible. This resulted in the creation of a massive state-owned industrial and services sector that brought with it specific dysfunctionalities, inefficiencies, cost disadvantages, and corporate governance problems.

The trend to limit private investment and foster inefficient manufacturing intensified during the late 1960s and early 1970s. The 1969 Monopolies and Restrictive Trade Practices Act linked industrial licensing with an assets-based classification of monopoly that applied only to the private sector. As a result private sector businesses whose assets exceeded a paltry amount varying from Rs.10 million to Rs1 billion had to apply for additional licenses to increase capacity, and more often than not, such applications were rejected. Widespread nationalization followed, beginning with insurance companies and banks, and then encompassing petroleum companies and collieries. One of the goals of nationalization was to preserve employment. Thus the 1970s and early 1980s saw successive governments taking over financially distressed private sector textile mills and engineering companies, thereby converting private bankruptcy to high-cost public debt.

In addition, the government made a fetish out of "small is beautiful." First, successive governments set up mini-plants, and the 1980s saw a mushrooming of technologically nonviable mini-steel, mini-cement, and mini-paper units whose profitability hinged on heavy tax concessions, high initial leveraging, subsidized long-term financing, high tariffs and import quotas, and the munificence of government orders. Second, the government actively encouraged small-scale industries. While this is not necessarily a bad thing— small and medium enterprises are often more efficient and flexible than larger firms—the small-scale sector was fostered through a plethora of artificial means, such as tax concessions and product reservations. Even today more than 800 product lines are reserved for the small-scale sector, of which more than 600 are not even manufactured in India.

Such distortions could not have existed in an outward-oriented, open economy. Despite preferential tariffs for the United Kingdom and other countries of the British empire, no major barriers to trade were in effect during the colonial era. Consequently, the major industries that had existed prior to independence (cotton textiles and yarn, jute, tea, and coal) were internationally competitive, and the jute and tea industries were driven by exports. Things began to change from the mid-1960s, intensifying with the import substituting regime of the 1970s and early 1980s. Import substitution made it incumbent upon a company to demonstrate to bureaucrats why any import was essential, and the doctrine of indigenous availability ensured the purchase of Indian inputs even when lower-quality products cost more than superior imports. Import substitution was sustained by quantitative restrictions, governed by various types of import licenses, and high tariffs. By 1985, the mean tariff rate was 146 percent for intermediate goods and 107 percent for capital goods.

While some of the policies certainly helped to establish industrial capacity, especially in engineering, drugs and pharmaceuticals, chemicals, fertilizers, and petrochemicals, they also created highly protected markets, fostered uncompetitiveness, and promoted large-scale rent-seeking, thereby providing fertile ground for corporate misgovernance.

Added to this was the corporate and personal income tax structure. At its peak, the corporate tax rate was as high as 55 percent and the maximum marginal rate for personal income tax was an astronomical 98.75 percent. Such rates created huge incentives for cheating, which took many forms, including undeclared cash perquisites, private expenses footed by company accounts, complicated emolument structures, and complex cross-holdings of shares to confound calculations regarding dividends and wealth taxes. The message was simple and profoundly negative. Thus what mattered was how to expropriate larger slices of a small pie, and how to do so in ways that escaped the tax net. Incentives to grow the pie, create wealth, and share it among stakeholders in transparent and equitable ways were completely lacking.

Following independence, the government set up three all-India development finance institutions (DFIs): the Industrial Finance Corporation of India, the Industrial Development Bank of India, and the Industrial Credit and Investment Corporation of India (ICICI). In addition, state governments set up state financial corporations. Until the early 1990s, the goal of these public sector DFIs was to foster industrialization by advancing long-term loans at low, often subsidized, real interest rates.

There is nothing wrong with a government with a fiscal surplus pushing subsidized long-term funds for creating competitive industrial capacities, as illustrated by the Republic of Korea's extensive industrial base. However, when careful project appraisal is abandoned for loan pushing—DFIs were evaluated on the basis of the number of loans approved and disbursed and not their asset quality—and when this occurs in a tightly controlled, rigidly licensed, highly protected, import-substituting milieu, it invariably results in crony capitalism, rent-seeking, inefficiency, and corporate misgovernance with public funds. This is precisely what occurred in India in the 1970s and 1980s.

The relationship between DFIs and corporation misgovernance has two aspects, one related to excess leveraging and the second with DFIs' role as shareholders. By the early 1980s, many term loans for industrial projects allowed project promoters to start projects with a relatively low equity base. During the industrial expansion of the 1970s and 1980s, the average share ownership of the controlling groups declined to 15 percent. In other words, it was possible to embark on a Rs500 million project with only Rs100 million of equity, of which a mere Rs15 million came from the promoters and sufficed for control. This set the state for moral hazard of limited liability. Given subsidized loan funds and various tax incentives to set up industries, most promoters recovered their relatively meager equity within a year or two of operation. Thereafter, in many cases after borrowers had recouped their outlay they failed to continue making loan repayments. The relationship between business groups and politicians ensured that defaulted debts would invariably be rescheduled in the name of rehabilitating financially sick industrial companies. Played out against the backdrop of inefficient implementation of bankruptcy laws, this created widespread corporate misgovernance, including a major diversion of DFI funds for other ventures.

With regard to shareholding, even now, nine years after the advent of economic liberalization, the DFIs, the nationalized insurance companies, and the government-owned mutual fund (the Unit Trust of India) hold a substantial portion of the equity of India's private sector companies. This kind of indirect state ownership of equity also fostered poor corporate governance through inefficient monitoring. The institutional shareholders insisted on nominating their directors to corporate boards; however, at best most of these nominee directors were incompetent; at worst they were instructed to support the incumbent management irrespective of its performance.

In theory, the three DFIs were well placed to play the role of corporate governance watchdogs in the 1970s and 1980s. If they had done their job well, they could have simultaneously reduced the agency costs associated with debt and equity, but they did not. On the equity side, the failure was related to the distorted incentives of government ownership and management of the DFls and the state-business nexus that induced directors to invariably vote with project promoters. On the debt side, it had much to do with inadequate income recognition and provisioning norms, as well as with poor bankruptcy and debt recovery procedures.

Thus by the time India embarked on economic liberalization, the waters had become muddied. On the one hand, the country had an equity base that was substantially greater than in most developing countries, had laws that regulated companies and protected the rights of shareholders, and had a large and active industrial sector ranging from complex petrochemicals to simple toy manufacturing. On the other hand, a combination of other factors had created an environment that did not punish poor corporate governance.

STRUCTURE OF CORPORATE INDIA

To understand the structure of India's corporate sector at the end of the 20th century, it is important to highlight the disruption that has been unleashed by less than a decade of economic liberalization. This has led to yesterday's giants, in many cases still family run, being dwarfed by the forces of change and being replaced by modern, professionally managed companies. Furthermore, economic liberalization, competitiveness, and the dismantling of controls have reduced entry barriers and permitted new entrepreneurs to race to the top of the market capitalization table. This trend away from family-run business to professionally-run businesses has augured well for corporate governance. The new breed of managers believes in professionalism and the credo of running businesses transparently to increase their corporate value. Thus the need for good corporate governance is being appreciated as a sound business strategy and as an important facilitator for tapping domestic and international capital.

India's corporate sector consists of closely held (private limited) and publicly held (public limited) companies, with the closely held companies vastly outnumbering the publicly held ones and constituting the bulk of small-scale enterprises; however, the public limited companies, including the listed ones, account for almost two thirds of the book value of equity. In addition the government corporate sector, while consisting of a mere 0.24 percent of the total number of companies in India accounts for 39 percent of paid-up capital. Finally, while India has 32 registered stock exchanges, many of them are moribund,[3] and only two really matter in terms of size, efficiency, and liquidity. These are the BSE and the National Stock Exchange, and any company with a good reputation is listed on one or the other, or even both. With a total of Rs10.3 trillion of market capitalization of companies listed on the two stock exchanges at the end of February 2002, the market capitalization of India's listed companies accounts for almost 53 percent of the country's gross domestic product. The BSE lists only 73 government companies, which accounts for less than 2 percent of the listing, yet these stocks account for almost 15 percent of market capitalization. This particular characteristic has important policy implications for corporate governance.

The Companies Act governs most corporations. This law is largely based on its British counterpart; however, many sections have been amended over time. In addition, the following three laws are also important from the point of view of corporate governance: The Securities Contracts (Regulation) Act of 1,956, the Securities and Exchange Board of India (SEBI) Act of 1992, and the Sick Industrial Companies (Special Provision) Act (SICA) of 1995.

AGENCY COSTS

Corporate ownership and control in Asia is characterized by three dominant themes. First, relative to their size, most Asian companies have low equity. Second, given the low equity base, promoters have found it relatively cheap to own majority shares. Third, equity ownership is invariably camouflaged through complex corporate cross-holdings.

These characteristics differentiate the Asian model from the U.S. corporate model of the 1970s and 1980s, with its large equity base, dispersed shareholdings, and profound separation of ownership from management. Agency costs are equally important in both models, but in the Asian model seem to affect minority shareholders' rights more than corporate efficiency. Under the Asian model a promoter who controls management and directly or indirectly owns more than 75 percent of a company's equity is not expected to perform in a value-destroying manner like many U.S. corporate managers and boards did up to the mid-1980s. However, promoters have the discretion to behave in a manner that deprives minority shareholders of their *de jure* ownership rights without adversely affecting a corporation's profits, including

---

[3] Many regional stock exchanges see no active trade whatsoever, and survive only on the basis of companies' annual listing fees.

by issuing preferential equity allotments to promoters and their allies at discounts or transferring shares through private buy-out deals at prices well below those prevailing in the secondary markets

Until the mid-1990s, India suffered from the worst of both types of agency costs. Dysfunctional economic and trade policies combined with low equity ownership to allow companies to thrive in uncompetitive ways, which became problematic when the economy started opening up to international competition. Corporate value eroded dramatically as measured in terms of economic value added, which is the difference between the return on capital employed and the opportunity cost of capital. However, ascertaining how much of this value destruction was due to poor corporate governance and how much was due to the companies' inertia and historical inability to deal with increased competition is difficult (Goswami, Karthikeyan, and Srivastava 1999).

Another problem was the expropriation of minority shareholder rights, facilitated in part by the nominee directors of banks, financial institutions, and DFIs, who invariably voted with management, and in part by inadequate legal provisions. For example, until seven years ago certain provisions of the Companies Act restricted the acquisition and transfer of shares. However, these provisions no longer apply, and a transparent legal framework is available for facilitating the market for equity-driven corporate control. In addition, transaction costs for trading shares have been reduced, allowing minority shareholders to enter and exit at will. Moreover, the market has begun to punish underperforming companies and those that disregard minority shareholders' interests.

DEBT AND EQUITY

While the market for corporate control has greatly improved on the equity side with a well-defined takeover code, the debt side remains as bad as it was during the days of control by licenses. The prevalence of widespread corporate misgovernance in countries with ineffective bankruptcy laws and procedures is not a coincidence. Poor protection of creditors' rights gives enormous—and ultimately deleterious—discretionary space to inefficient management. It allows companies to reallocate funds to highly risky investments, given that the management fears neither attachment nor bankruptcy; it needlessly raises the cost of credit; it debases the disciplining role of debt; and it eventually ruins the health of a country's financial sector. Unfortunately, India has poor bankruptcy reorganization laws and procedures, and its liquidation procedures are even worse.

Bankruptcy

The reorganization of insolvent large industrial companies is governed by the SICA, directed and supervised by the Board for Financial and Industrial Reconstruction (BIFR). Five fundamental flaws of poorly designed and inadequately implemented bankruptcy procedures are associated with the SICA-BIFR process, namely:

- *Late detection.* The law defines financial distress as the erosion of net worth. This is much worse than bankruptcy, which is basically a default on debt. When a company loses so much as to erode its net worth, the probability of a successful turnaround is low. Not surprisingly, between July 1987 and November 1998 only 11 percent of the 1,954 cases that BIFR considered "maintainable" have recovered.
- *Cumbersome and time-consuming procedures.* Between 1987 and 1992 the BIRF took an average of 851 days to arrive at a decision, and since then the average delay has doubled. The delay is caused by extensive quasi-judicial procedures whereby cases go through multiple loops before a final decision is taken. Naturally, such delays confer additional bargaining power to the management of the bankrupt company at the expense of secured and senior creditors.
- *Indefinite stay on all claims of creditors.* From the time a company is registered as bankrupt until the case is disposed of, the BIFR does not allow creditors to exercise any claims. All reasonable restructuring processes confer time-bound stays, but the BIFR's excessive delays make such legal stays a key strategic device for the promoters of debtor firms. All they need to do is to get the case registered, which then protects them from creditors' claims for at least four years.
- *Debtor in possession.* Neither SICA nor BIFR recognize that incumbent management always has a significant informational advantage compared with outside creditors. Therefore a procedure that allows existing management to control and run a bankrupt company during the period when it is being reorganized invariably results in secured creditors taking major hits on their exposures at the expense of shareholders and management.
- *Violation of the absolute priority rule.* This rule states that in any bankruptcy restructuring or liquidation process, the claims of senior creditors have to be settled in full before those of junior creditors are considered. BIFR's procedures violate this principal by often rewarding incumbent management and incumbent shareholders at the expense of fully secured creditors.

Designing a far better bankruptcy reorganization system is not difficult. The key features of a market-driven and incentive-compatible procedure would incorporate the following features:

- The definition of bankruptcy should be altered to debt default. This will result in earlier detection of financial distress and increase the likelihood of a successful turnaround.
- Up to a point, bankruptcy restructuring should be voluntary. The onus must be on the company to convince its secured and senior creditors with a satisfactory rescheduling and cash flow plan.
- The case should only be taken to the BIRF if negotiations between the company and senior creditors break down. If this additional time for negotiation does not succeed, the BIFR should appoint an independent administrator to advertise the sale of the company. During the advertising and sale period, the BIFR should impose a strictly time-bound stay on creditors' claims on the company's assets. In the meanwhile, an independent financial professional can determine the company's liquidation value, which will serve as the confidential reserve price.
- The sealed bid offers must be submitted within the given time period. During this period, subject to a confidentiality bond, all prospective bidders should be permitted to conduct due diligence. Existing promoters can also bid.
- The bids should be in two parts: (a) the post-restructuring profit and loss account, balance sheet, and cash flow projections; and (b) the financial bid, which can be in cash or in recognized securities.
- Secured and senior creditors should vote within their class on (a). Those bids that secure the assent of 75 percent of secured and senior credit should be short-Iisted. The best financial bid from the short-list is the winning bid.
- If the winning bid amounts to less than the liquidation value, then the company should go into liquidation. If it is greater than the liquidation value, but less than the secured debt, then the proceeds should be prorated across secured creditors (including wage dues), with unsecured creditors getting nothing.

Under such an arrangement the BIFR would act as a facilitator instead of behaving like a court. Such a scheme was laid down in the 1997 Sick Industrial Companies Bill, but political instability has kept the bill in limbo.

Liquidation

If bankruptcy restructuring under the BIFR is tedious, liquidation under the Companies Act is virtually impossible. High court delays in winding up companies that are beyond redemption take up to 10 years for most cases, but have been known to take as long as 50 years. These delays illustrate the failure (a) to understand that preserving the value of a company's assets is of primary importance, and that this is best achieved by ensuring that these assets are quickly reallocated to productive use by more efficient entrepreneurs; and (b) to realize that those most severely affected by delays are employees and secured creditors.

In 1996 – 1997 the Working Group on the Companies Act recommended an entirely new approach to this problem with the following key features:

- Encouraging voluntary winding up
- Separating the two aspects of liquidation by selling assets first and then distributing the proceeds
- Laying down a coherent description of the steps that have to be taken along with the order in which they have to be taken and time frames for each action
- Explaining how the act would catalyze a rapid, transparent, and market-determined sale of assets
- Laying down well-defined and non-subjective norms to ascertain whether a company's assets should be sold in their entirety as a going concern or in parts
- Permitting professionals, such as chartered accountants, lawyers, or company secretaries, to act as company liquidators.

However, none of these proposals have been adopted to date.

By law, creditors have prior claims over shareholders. When their contractual obligations are not adhered to, creditors can do one of three things: demand a bankruptcy reorganization under SICA/BIFR auspices, file for a winding up of the company, or apply for receivership. The first two options do not constitute credible threats. As for the speed with which creditors can obtain a receivership decree, this varies. The process is relatively efficient in Murnbai, extremely inefficient bordering on impossible in Calcutta, and somewhere in between elsewhere.

Since 1993 banks and DFIs have had recourse to the option of filing for recovery of debts through debt recovery tribunals. These quasi-judicial bodies were set up in response to inordinate delays in the judicial system. However, the tribunals have their own problems. Many of them have not yet been established, and those that have been established have become backlogged.

Thus in reality, creditors have little protection. A consequence of this is extreme risk aversion, especially in the new milieu where public sector bank managers have to stop pushing loans and focus on their bottom line. As a result, banks are in a peculiar situation. On the one hand, they are flush with depositors' funds. On the other, they avoid lending to anyone other than blue chip companies and invest the remainder in Treasury bills, which are risk free, do not impair their capital adequacy, give a return that is at least 300 basis points above the average deposit rate, and, most important, require no effort at project appraisal. This pervasive debasing of debt is choking off funds to small and medium enterprises, and unless rectified by better implementation of creditors' rights will have serious negative implications for the future structure and sustainability of industrial growth.

Equity-Driven Takeovers

The SEBI, established in 1992, has significantly reformed the equity side of the market for corporate control. Until the introduction of the Takeover Code in 1997, companies could negotiate takeover deals that frequently left minority shareholders in the lurch. The code now regulates various aspects of share purchases. This has had two beneficial effects. First, it has created a transparent market for takeovers. Second, it has ensured that minority shareholders have the right to obtain a market-driven price in any takeover. Furthermore, in the case of a growing number of attempts of hostile takeovers, it has proved to be a robust instrument.

DISCLOSURE

According to the law, all companies must prepare audited annual accounts that are first submitted to the company's board for approval, then sent to all the shareholders, and finally provided to the registrar of companies. Listed companies must also submit their annual accounts to every stock exchange on which they are listed, prepare unaudited financial summaries for every quarter, and submit a cash flow statement. In theory, companies' most substantive financial disclosures are to be found in their annual reports, especially their balance sheets, profit and loss statements, and relevant schedules.

Balance sheets have to address both sources of funds as well as their application. With regard to the sources of funds, the reporting on secured loans, which includes a full line-by-line disclosure of debentures, is most problematic. Unfortunately, Indian accounting standards do not follow the principle of consolidation, and as a result companies can, and do, under- or overstate such transactions for strategic purposes. With regard to the application of funds, the quality of disclosure of fixed assets could be significantly improved by introducing the evaluation of all elements at either market price *or* historical cost, and by allowing for deferred tax liability. The disclosure of investments is an area that allows for most opaqueness, because investments in quoted and unquoted securities are evaluated in different ways. A possible solution to this problem could be to mandate consolidation according to U.S. Generally Accepted Accounting Principles or Internationally Accepted Accounting Standards and by insisting on full disclosure of all related party transactions.

Disclosure required in the profit and loss account is quite exhaustive and mostly corresponds to international standards. There are, however, two areas that can be misused. The first relates to manufacturing expenses, which can be inflated up to the point where it requires collusion with the government's sales tax and excise duty officials. The second has to do with sales, distribution, administration, and other expenses. However, the scope for misreporting on these two heads is far less than for some items on the balance sheet.

As far as incorporated companies go, the standards for financial disclosure in their annual accounts are better than prevailing standards in most of Asia; however, until 2001–2002 they were not in line with U.S. and international norms. While the Companies Act specifies punishments for noncompliance with financial disclosure requirements, these are light. In most instances the maximum penalty is either six months' imprisonment, a fine of no more than Rs2000 ($48), or both. In practice, few people have been imprisoned and the system is relatively lax. For instance, if the auditor's signed reports are not in conformity with the law, the maximum penalty is Rs1,000 (US$24). Lengthy judicial delays further diminish the minimal deterrence provided by such penalties. Moreover, some ethically questionable acts are considered normal. For instance, while the Institute of Chartered Accountants of India prescribes detailed standards for external auditors, it has rarely taken any serious action against its members. Stock markets are carrying out their own enforcement. Increasingly, companies are enjoying premiums for good corporate disclosure, which has increased the demand for internationally respected and independent audit firms, especially when companies are seeking access to foreign capital. This might clean up the system faster than legally mandated enforcement.

Since the early 1990s companies must be rated by approved credit rating agencies before issuing any commercial paper, bonds, or debentures. India currently has five rating agencies, four of which are well established. Each agency has a set of ratings that ranges from extremely safe to poorer than junk bond status. Ratings have to be made public, and must be accompanied by the rating agencies' perceptions of risk factors that can affect the payment of interest and the repayment of principal. Company management has the right to comment on these risk factors. In the past companies have tended to "ratings shop," that is, to approach more than one rating agency and then publish the most favorable rating. The Confederation of Indian Industry is attempting to rectify this situation by mandating that companies reveal if they have been rated by more than one credit rating agency and to provide the ratings as determined by each agency. The three all-India DFIs hold stock in three of the credit rating agencies. Recently, SEBI has mandated that these agencies not be allowed to rate any companies in which the DFIs hold stock or their subsidiaries.

The Companies Act requires all companies to maintain a register of shareholders that must be updated whenever shares change hands. Even though the register is legally public domain information and a list of shareholders must be sent to the registrar of companies, in practice it is not as public as it is made out to be, especially for closely held, unlisted companies. Accessing shareholding information for listed companies is easier. Stock exchange listing agreements require a breakdown of shares by individual promoters, DFIs, foreign institutional investors, mutual funds, foreign holdings, other corporate bodies, top 50 shareholders, and other shareholders. However, this classification often fails to give a fully transparent picture of share control because of the prevalence of complex cross-holdings across most conglomerates controlled by a family or group. The objective of such cross-holdings within traditional family-dominated businesses, which constitute a sizable proportion of listed companies, was to avoid the steep wealth and inheritance taxes that characterized pre-1991 India. Abolition of both these taxes and the tax on individuals' dividend income, along with a reduction in personal income tax rates, has led many such businesses to slowly unwind their cross-holdings. The process of moving toward cleaner and more transparent share ownership is also being driven by an increasingly active stock market. Foreign institutional investors, who now account for 24 to 30 percent of the equity of highly traded companies, avoid companies with complex cross-holdings. Another factor that has diminished the importance of cross-holdings is the meteoric rise of new, technologically-oriented companies. Today, two internationally recognized information technology companies and eight drug companies are among India's leading firms. These enterprises are run along highly professional lines.

While the 1992 SEBI Act clearly defines insider trading and states that one of the functions of the capital market regulator is to prohibit insider trading, as in most countries the problem lies in implementation. Even with sophisticated detection devices, pinpointing insider trades is extremely difficult. In the United States fewer than 1 percent of the trades that are initially identified as potential cases of insider trading are actually investigated, and fewer still result in convictions. In India, in addition to this same difficulty of flagging possible cases of insider trading, two additional problems are apparent. First, given the large number of brokers and middlemen who operate in the market, people with insider information can create enough firewalls between themselves and the traders to make identifying the real insiders extremely difficult. Second, while SEBI can conduct an investigation, prepare a report, and even suggest a penalty, it lacks the judicial power to impose that penalty. Only the courts can impose penalties, and given the judicial delays, such penalties carry little weight. Nevertheless, SEBI has investigated several cases of insider trading, primarily, but not exclusively, involving relatively small players.

Although Indian banks and DFIs disclose more than their counterparts in East and Southeast Asia and, indeed, Switzerland, this is still considerably less than what is desirable. In particular, neither banks nor DFIs are required to disclose the structure and extent of any asset-liability mismatch. Moreover, while they follow the Basle standards for recognition of non-performing assets, this does not take into account some of the institutional realities of India, for example, the length of time taken for cases involving bad loans to be resolved. In this context, ICICI has taken the lead. Driven by the objective of becoming India's first truly universal bank, ICICI has decided to tap the US capital market. To this end it voluntarily re-cast its accounts for the fiscal year ended 31 March 1999 in terms of US generally accepted accounting principles. While the exercise eroded ICICI's bottom line by a third, it also created investor confidence.

BOARDS OF DIRECTORS

Perhaps the greatest drawback of corporate governance in India is the de facto lack of independent directors on the vast majority of boards. This is not caused by a lack of supply, but reflects the lack of demand, given the prevailing attitude that boards are empty legal constructs that exist solely to justify the perpetuation of existing management.

While corporate law clearly stipulates the requirements for a board of directors and states that all directors are fiduciaries of the shareholders, most boards do not satisfy any of the conditions that accompany the principle of independent oversight. For example, there is no legal definition of independence in relation to directors, and nonexecutive directors tend to account for no more than one third of the total number of board members and often play a passive role. In public sector banks in particular, in they often do not understand their responsibilities and have little specialized knowledge, and thus do not use their position to exercise effective oversight. Agendas for board meetings rarely provide adequate information or are distributed sufficiently in advance of board meetings; board meetings are often scheduled for a short duration; and until recently there was no law or regulation that required boards to establish audit, remuneration, or nomination committees. All this reflects a basic malaise of the corporate sector whereby most companies are driven by their management and not by their boards.

How can one make the boards of Indian companies more active and interested in maximizing shareholder value? To begin with, measures could be taken to create the right kind of environment, for example, by raising directors' remuneration beyond the ceiling of Rs5,000 ($115) per meeting, which is hardly sufficient compensation for properly exercising fiduciary responsibilities, and by offering a commission on net profits and stock options to stimulate directors' interest in maximizing corporate value. In addition, listed companies should be mandated to disclose directors' attendance records in their annual reports. While attendance is not a proxy for performance, shareholders are likely to be more reluctant to re-elect directors who fail to attend meetings regularly than those who do.

Despite these criticisms, major changes are occurring in the boards of the top 20 or 30 private sector companies. Most have a majority of non-executive directors (if not genuinely independent ones), have at least an audit committee, and pay a commission to directors over and above their token sitting fees, and some are contemplating stock options. They send the right kind of agenda papers well in advance of board meetings, and board meetings last longer than a few hours.

STATE-OWNED ENTERPRISES

State-owned enterprises (SOEs) account for 20 percent of market capitalization among listed companies. Shareholders of private sector companies are the direct beneficiaries of profitable performance, and thus in theory have an incentive to monitor management so that it maximizes corporate value. In contrast, most SOEs, especially unlisted SOEs, do not have a substantial body of informed private shareholders whose income depends upon the performance of these companies. If anything, the major shareholder of SOEs has distinctly different objectives. The typical member of Parliament or minister is rarely concerned about commercial viability, profitability, quality, cost minimization, optimal investment decisions, and corporate value creation. As for civil servants, they are trained to slavishly adhere to procedures, however irrelevant such procedures may be.

In other words, governments and their agents are process oriented, whereas enterprises should be results oriented. This mismatch is further exacerbated by civil servants' aversion to risk taking. Thus when civil servants serve on the board of an SOE, they typically toe the ministry line, ensure that the SOE follows "proper" procedures, and avoid any risky decisions that may have harmful consequences for their ministries. Thus most chief executives of SOEs quickly adopt the line of least resistance. As a result important organizational changes are not made, poorly performing staff remain on the payroll, loss-making plants are neither downsized nor closed, wages are not linked to productivity, and excess workers are not let go.

State ownership has had a number of negative impacts, for example, all SOEs are expected to achieve a number of noncommercial objectives that are defined by the state and must adhere to affirmative action norms for employment to ensure that the percentage of representation of certain groups (scheduled castes and tribes, the handicapped, former members of the military, and so on) is equal to that in central government ministries. In addition, because of pressure from the comptroller and accountant general's annual audit, they are inclined to accept the lowest bidder for procurement tenders, even when quality is poor, and they have little autonomy in making major decisions, including the appointment of senior management personnel or financial investments.

As the current government recognizes, the only solution to these issues is systematic and transparent privatization of the SOEs. However, progress to this end has been poor, partly because of resistance from the entrenched, rent-seeking bureaucracy, and partly because of the lack of sufficient political will. In the meantime the SOEs are losing corporate value and their best managers are leaving for jobs in the private sector.

RECENT CORPORATE GOVERNANCE INITIATIVES

Two major corporate governance initiatives have been launched in India since the mid-1990s, the first has been by the Confederation of Indian Industry, India's largest industry and business association, and the second by SEBI. More than a year before the onset of the 1997 Asian crisis the Confederation of Indian Industry set up a committee to examine corporate governance issues and recommend a voluntary code of best practices. The committee released "Desirable Corporate Governance: A Code" in April 1998 (see http://www.ciionline.org/busserv/corporate/backup/cgcode.htm). The code focuses on listed companies and provides detailed recommendations that address the items identified earlier.

As for the functioning of boards of directors, the code recommends, for instance, the appointment of a core group of knowledgeable and professionally acclaimed nonexecutive directors; a minimum number of board meetings per year; the nonaccumulation of executive positions by one person; the payment of a commission to directors based on corporate performance and the provision of stock options; and the establishment of annual operating plans and budgets, accompanied by updated long-term plans. The code further recommends providing boards of directors with details of any joint ventures or collaboration agreements; information about transactions that involve substantial payment for goodwill, brand equity, or intellectual property; and information on the recruitment and remuneration of senior officers. In addition, the code recommends the establishment of audit committees. The code also makes recommendations with regard to disclosure of various aspects of companies' performance and staff, including the rating received from all credit rating agencies.

These efforts have started to bear fruit. For the financial year ended 31 March 1999, 23 large, listed companies accounting for 19 percent of India's market capitalization fully or partly adopted these disclosure norms. A more subtle effect of the initiative has been that companies have tended to look more positively at the concept of corporate governance rather than dismissing it as a passing fad.

The other major corporate governance initiative was taken by SEBI starting in early 1999. By early 2000 SEBI had prepared a number of mandated recommendations that apply to listed companies and are to be enforced at the level of stock exchanges through listing agreements (see http://www.sebi.com). Similar to the code drafted by the Confederation of Indian Industry, these recommendations cover such issues as board composition, define the notion of independent directors and the kind of information that needs to be provided to shareholders, and recommend the establishment of an independent audit committee at the board level. The recommendations furthermore define a number of disclosure requirements. These recommendations are to be implemented following a timetable. All companies listing for the first time must adhere to these recommendations at the time of listing. For companies that are already listed, depending on their share capital and/or net worth, they had to be in compliance by 31 March 2001 or 2002, or must be in compliance no later than 31 March 2003.

While most of SEBI's recommendations follow from the Confederation of Indian Industry's code, SEBI's mandate clearly has more teeth, in that unlike the code, it is not voluntary but mandatory. However, some issues raise concerns. One such issue is that of assuring compliance. While delisting is a credible threat for larger companies, this is not the case for the vast majority of listed companies that have little floating stock. A second issue is the fear that by legally mandating several aspects of corporate governance, SEBI might unintentionally encourage the practice of companies managing by means of checklists instead of focusing on the spirit of good governance.

This raises a question of what should be voluntary and what should be mandatory. In an ideal world with efficient capital markets such a question would not arise, because the market would distinguish between well-run companies and poorly-run companies and reward and punish them accordingly. Unfortunately, ideal capital markets exist only in theory. Thus what is needed is a small corpus of legally mandated rules, buttressed by a much larger body of self-regulation and voluntary compliance. This will no doubt happen in India. When all listed companies are forced to follow the SEBI guidelines, the better firms will voluntarily raise the bar so as to be measured according to best international practices in an effort to attract international funds.

CONCLUSION

While corporate governance has been slow in making its mark in India, the next few years will see a flurry of activity. This will be driven by several factors as follows:

- The increased competition to which corporate India has been exposed since the mid-1990s has forced companies to drastically restructure their management practices.
- There has been a major shift in company pecking order, with young companies managed by modern, outward oriented professionals who place a great deal of value on corporate governance and transparency clawing their way to the top.
- There has been a phenomenal growth in market capitalization, which has resulted in a fundamental change in mindset whereby creating and distributing wealth has become a rather popular maxim.
- Foreign investors have repeatedly demanded better corporate governance, more transparency, and greater disclosure, and have made this requirement felt by increasing their exposure in well-governed firms at the expense of poorly run ones. The same can be said for foreign pension funds, which are likely to increase in importance in the coming years.
- An increasingly strong financial press has induced a new level of disclosure, both with regard to companies' financial statements and to internal governance matters.
- Banks and DFIs are no longer willing to support management irrespective of performance. The tendency of more market-oriented DFIs to start converting some of their outstanding debt to equity and to set up mergers and acquisition subsidiaries to sell their shares in underperforming companies to more dynamic groups will further intensify over time.
- It is widely recognized among Indian corporations that improving corporate governance and applying internationally accepted accounting and disclosure standards is likely to facilitate access to U.S. capital markets.
- In a few more years India will have moved to full capital account convertibility. This will increase Indian investors' freedom to choose between Indian and foreign companies for placing their funds, and good corporate governance will be one of the major issues that these investors will consider.

Given these developments, the prediction that by the end of 2005 India might have the largest concentration of well-governed companies in South and Southeast Asia may well come to pass.

REFERENCES

Goswami, Omkar. 1996. Legal and Institutional Impediments to Corporate Growth. In *Policy Reform in India,* edited by Charles Oman. Paris: OECD, Development Centre.

Omkar Goswami, M. Karthikeyan, and G. Srivastava. 1999. Are Indian Companies Losing Shareholder Value? *Confederation of Indian Industry Corporate Research Series* 1 (1).

E. The Role of the Judiciary: Improving the Investigation and Prosecution of Bribery

Chapter 10

Focus Group Study of Factors That Could Help Improve the Investigation and Prevention of Corruption in Indonesia

■ **Narayanan Srinivasan**

This chapter discusses issues in relation to corruption taking into account the three pillars of action formulated as part of the Action Plan for the Asia–Pacific region.

THEORETICAL FRAMEWORK

The theoretical framework for most forms of corruption and white-collar crimes was set by Sutherland in 1939, when he introduced the term white-collar crime (Sutherland 1983). (For the purpose of this chapter I argue that the kinds of corruption we face in this region falls within the category of white-collar crimes.) Sutherland's theory put forward the notion that criminal behavior is learned behavior. In simple terms, Sutherland's theory of differential association classifies all forms of criminal behavior as learned and copied. Public officials learn to be corrupt by observing their coworkers and justifying their acts as being normal behavior in their particular environments.

Box, another prominent criminologist, adds the element of skills and opportunity as being the major motivating factors behind white-collar criminals (Box 1983). Skills are developed by observing coworkers, and when the opportunity presents itself, these skills are activated to commit a crime.

In order to prevent corruption, those charged with investigating and preventing it should understand these theories, which help identify both the causes of corruption and the personalities of people who engage in it.

INDONESIAN STUDY OF PERSONNEL INVOLVED IN INVESTIGATING CORRUPTION AND BRIBERY

The Indonesian study offered an opportunity to put into practice an innovative methodology to improve the investigation and prevention of corruption. It was based on sound methodology aimed at meeting a set of specific criteria.

Methodology

The study was based on a methodology of critical hermeneutics (Crofty 1998; Rundell 1991; Warnke 1987), which uses focus groups to ensure that individuals from different countries and/or institutions participate in the learning process leading to their own development. This methodology also provides the impetus for local participants to take ownership of issues and think through and identify their own situations as discussed and analyzed during and after the focus group meetings (Bernstein 1983; Zemke 1998). Five focus group meetings were held during a period of 18 months. Each meeting consisted of four separate groups of participants, who were mid-level and senior officers from the various agencies (police, judiciary, regulators, private sector, and others) involved in investigating corruption and bribery in Indonesia. The first group meeting was attended by 41 people who were selected based on recommendations from various government and private sector agencies. The main criteria in selecting this group were that they were mid-level or senior officers and had at least seven years' experience of investigating corruption-related activities. A decision was made to include people who had worked in the private sector after discussions with the local partners of this project, who felt that personnel employed by the private sector (mainly multinational companies) to investigate corrupt practices would contribute positively to these groups. Such people (and a small number of observers) attended subsequent group meetings. All groups had above 80 percent attendance.

Three weeks before the first meeting, all focus group participants were given materials to read about issues relating to corruption (see the reference list and bibliography for an idea of the types of materials provided to the participants). All the participants were also asked to think about how they could help improve the framework for investigating corruption and what changes, if any, they would recommend for making their respective jobs easier and more effective. They were also given a brief outline of how the project would function and an introduction to critical hermeneutics and the logistics of the focus group meetings.

At the first focus group meeting, a series of questions was formulated by the four working groups, and their leaders generated a list of factors relevant to these questions from each group. Further focus group meetings were based on this list of factors. At the second meeting specific themes were identified and the groups were divided into four thematic clusters. Leaders from each of the clusters drew up a final list of factors that the participants had identified as ones that would help improve the investigation and prosecution of corruption-related offenses. At all stages the participants were assured of absolute confidentiality.

Major Findings

The findings of this study are preliminary, as the final report has been disseminated to all the participants for their comments.

The first and second focus group meetings identified five themes as being of utmost importance for enabling the effective investigation of corruption, namely:

- Legislation
- Training
- Interagency cooperation
- Public awareness
- Effective implementation.

LEGISLATION. Focus group one discussed the adequacy of current legislation, the judiciary, and the process of influencing government. This group raised the following main points:

- The current legislation relating to many aspects of investigating and prosecuting corruption-related activities is adequate, with two exceptions, that is, money laundering and political interference. The group felt strongly that international efforts should concentrate on strengthening these omissions as they were beyond their control.
- The group identified the independence of the judiciary as an issue separate from the adequacy of legislation. Most of the participants agreed that the existence of good legislation and the implementation

of good legislation are quite separate issues. This group implied that in Indonesia, the legislation in relation to anti-corruption investigation and prosecution is good, but because of issues relating to the judiciary, the implementation of this legislation is the real problem. Judicial independence would also help reduce corruption (Ades and Tella 1996; Gurgur and Shah 2000).

• The group also highlighted political interference in decisionmaking about anti-corruption investigations. The participants felt that even though political interference did exist, it was not as rampant as reported in the international media. They identified political will as the issue that must be addressed and as being much more important than political interference. After much discussion, the group defined political will as the ability of the political mechanism (both governmental and private) to identify corrupt activities and be sincere about rooting out corruption at all levels.

TRAINING. Focus group two discussed issues relating to training officials working in both private and governmental organizations investigating and prosecuting corruption. The issues this group identified are as follows:

• A concentrated and coordinated training effort by both the Indonesian government and international agencies is lacking. The participants felt that the many ad hoc training initiatives being undertaken by the various international agencies and coordinated by the government did not meet the needs of the people concerned. All the participants had attended training programs (most had attended at least two in the past 24 months) organized by international agencies and foreign governments in areas related to anti-corruption. While they noted that many of these programs were excellent in content and presentation, most of them did not address local needs and legislation.

• The participants also identified the lack of specific programs that would be helpful in an international context. As an example, the activities of the Financial Actions Task Force had been explained to one of the participants, the only one afforded this explanation in an entire organization actively involved in investigating money laundering and asset tracing.

• The participants also identified a need for specific skills training in areas related to legislation and investigation to improve the investigation of corruption. All the participants felt that this would improve their rate of success in investigating corruption, as currently Indonesia has only a handful of highly trained corruption investigators.

INTERAGENCY COOPERATION. Focus group three, which concentrated on interagency cooperation, believed that despite the many initiatives—such as the Jakarta Initiative, the Corporate Governance Initiative, the Anti-Corruption Plan, and the Ombudsmen's Office—the question of interagency cooperation has not been addressed. The main recommendations this group made include the following:

- A special task force should be established to map the types of interagency cooperation that would be workable in the Indonesian environment. This task force should take into account the work the many local and provincial government agencies are undertaking. The task force should also look into the legislative changes that would be required to make interagency cooperation function easily.
- As concerned international agencies, nongovernment organizations (NGOs), and other agencies involved in investigating corruption, the group identified many international agencies and NGOs that seemed to be working in isolation, because the current environment in Indonesia does not encourage cooperative arrangements.
- Within the Indonesian criminal justice system, the various agencies working in the area of corruption investigation and prosecution are not required to work together. The group identified many informal links, but felt that a more formal approach of mandated meetings between private and government officials would improve overall effectiveness.

PUBLIC AWARENESS. Focus group four discussed public awareness and identified the following major issues:

- A concentrated public awareness campaign is needed on the negative effects that corruption has on an economy. The group agreed that in most cases the participants had investigated, both the victims and the perpetrators had extensive knowledge about corruption and white-collar crime. In many instances the people they had investigated understood clearly that they had broken the law, but argued that their actions did not hurt anyone.
- The role that the public should play in preventing corruption should also be publicized. The group noted that in Indonesia many NGOs play an active role in corruption prevention. One major activity that these NGOs could undertake is spreading the word about the importance of informants and whistleblowers in corruption identification and prevention. The participants stressed that the role

of the public is important not only in preventing corruption, but also in investigating it. They cited many examples of cases where the informants were unaware of their rights and where employers victimized whistleblowers. The participants identified some public awareness campaigns that had been carried out by organizations such as the International Committee against Corruption in Hong Kong, China, and felt that these campaigns should be adapted for Indonesia.

- The group believed that education on corruption and investigation of corrupt activities, including the roles of agencies involved in investigation, should be disseminated to the employees of all government and private organizations. Again, they identified Hong Kong, China, as a good example and the most appropriate for the Indonesian context.

- The role of educating the young was another area where the participants believed that funds could be directed. They felt that it was not their role to define or identify ways that this could be done (as they were mostly senior members of investigative agencies), but stressed the importance of this activity.

Overall, all the participants agreed that the examples from Hong Kong, China, which had been provided as part of their preparation for this project (Fee-Man 1999), seemed to be the most appropriate for the Indonesian environment. If these could be expanded to the provinces and local governments, it would help in the investigation of corruption and white-collar crimes.

IMPLEMENTATION. All the participants agreed that the most pressing issue facing them, as either senior investigators or directors of investigative agencies, was to implement good investigative practices. As noted earlier, critical hermeneutics is a method that would create an understanding of the issues and bring about a questioning of "what is." The implementation issue raised by this group is just another step closer to an understanding of what needs to be done. The group did not offer any solutions, even after intensive discussions, except to note the need for significant resources to improve the working conditions and training provided by the government to these investigators and their staff.

CONCLUSION

Using the Action Plan's three pillars as a guide and critical hermeneutics as the methodology, we can conclude that international agencies need to help

Indonesian investigative agencies (governmental, quasi-governmental, and private) implement good investigative approaches. The focus group study provides a starting point that indicates what senior investigators and their managers working in the government and in private agencies in Indonesia have identified as their needs to increase the success rate of their investigations.

One interesting point that this group raised during discussions was their perception of the West's preoccupation with processes rather than outcomes. As an example, the participants felt that in many instances, the final outcomes in selecting successful bidders for projects would have been the same, but the process became so complicated that this process itself gave rise to opportunities for engaging in corrupt behavior. Again no solution was discussed, but the participants raised this as an issue that international organizations and multinationals should consider when insisting on tendering for small projects.

REFERENCES AND BIBLIOGRAPHY

Ades, A., and R. Di Tella. 1995. Competition and Corruption. *Oxford Applied Economics Discussion Paper Series* 169 (April): 18.

_____. 1997. The Causes and Consequences of Competition: A Review of Recent Empirical Contributions. In B. Harris-White and G. White, eds., *Liberalization and the New Corruption*. Institute of Development Studies Bulletin 27(2):6-11.

Albonetti, C. A. 1994. The Symbolic Punishment of White-Collar Offenders." In G. S. Bridges and M. A. Myers, eds., *Inequality, Crime, and Social Control*. Boulder, Colorado: Westview Press.

Ayres, I., and J. Braithwaite. 1991. Tripartism: Regulatory Capture and Empowerment. *Law & Social Inquiry* (16): 435-96.

Barak, G. 1991. *Crimes by the Capitalist State: An Introduction to State Criminality*. Albany, New York: SUNY Press.

Bernstein, R. 1983. *Beyond Objectivism and Realism: Science, Hermeneutics, and Praxis*. Philadelphia: University of Pennsylvania Press.

Breed, B. 1979. *White-Collar Bird*. London: John Clare.

Box, Steven. 1983. *Power, Crime, and Mystification*. London: Tavistock.

Crofty, M. 1998. *The Foundations of Social Research: Meaning and Perspective in Research Process*. Australia: Allen and Unwin.

Cullen, F., B. Link, L. Travis, and J. Wozniak. 1985. Consensus in Crime Seriousness: Empirical Reality or Methodological Artifact? *Criminology* 23(1): 99-119.

Evans, P. B., and S. A. Schneider. 1981. The Political Economy of the Corporation. In S. G. McNall, ed., *Political Economy: A Critique of American Society.* Glenview, Illinois: Scott, Foresman.

Evans, T. D., E. T. Cullen, and P. J. Dubeck. 1993. Public Perception of Corporate Crime. In M. B. Blankenship, ed., *Understanding Corporate Criminality.* New York: Garland.

Fee-Man, Julie Mu. 1999. Hong Kong, China's Anti-Corruption Strategy. In *Combating Corruption in Asian and Pacific Economies,* ADB, Manila, 2000, 227-232.

Friedland, M. L., ed. 1990. *Securing Compliance: Seven Case Studies.* Toronto: University of Toronto Press.

Geis, G. 1984 White-Collar and Corporate Crime. In R. Meier, ed., *Major Forms of Crime.* Beverly Hills, California: Sage.

Glazer, M. P., and P. M. Glazer. 1989. *The Whistleblowers.* New York: Basic Books.

Goldstein, H. 1975. *Police Corruption.* Washington, DC: Police Foundation.

Gurgur, Tugrul, and Anwar Shah. 1999. Major Causes of Corruption. Working Paper Series no. 2054. World Bank, Washington, DC.

_____. 2000. Localization and Corruption: Panacea or a Pandora's Box. Paper presented at the International Monetary Fund Conference on Fiscal Decentralization, 21 November, Washington, DC.

Ling, E. 1991. Fraud and Social Change: Whistleblowing and White-Collar Crime in a Major Corporation. Ph.D. dissertation, Ohio State University.

Makkai, T., and J. Braithwaite. 1994. Reintegrative Shaming and Compliance with Regulatory Standards. *Criminology* 32: 361-86.

Malec, K., and J. Gardiner. 1987. Measurement Issues in the Study of Official Corruption: A Chicago Example. *Corruption and Reform* 2: 267-78.

Rundell, J. 1991. *Social Theory: A Guide to Central Thinkers.* Australia: Allen & Unwin.

Sutherland, E. 1983. *White-Collar Crime: The Uncut Version.* London: Yale University Press.

Schacter, Mark, and Anwar Shah. 2000. Anti-Corruption Programs: Look before You Leap. Paper prepared for the International Conference on Corruption, December, Seoul, Republic of Korea.

Smith, R. 1982. *Learning How to Learn: Applied Theory for Adults.* Chicago: Follett.

Warnke, G. 1987. *Gadamer: Hermeneutics, Tradition, and Reason.* Cambridge, UK: Polity Press.

Zemke, R. 1998 In Search of Self Directed Learners. *Training* (May): 60-68.

Chapter 11

Role of Public Prosecutors in Japan

■ **Yuichiro Tachi**

In Japan attorneys, judges, and public prosecutors have the same qualifications, therefore, the status of public prosecutors is equivalent to that of judges and they receive equal salaries depending on the length of time they have held their positions. Their independence and impartiality are also protected by law. Aside from disciplinary proceedings, they cannot be dismissed from office, suspended from the performance of their duties, or be forced to accept a reduced salary.

The duties of public prosecutors include carrying out investigations, instituting prosecutions, ensuring that the courts apply the law correctly, and ensuring that judgments have been carried out. In addition, many public prosecutors are assigned to key positions in the Ministry of Justice, for example, as vice-minister of justice and director-general of the Criminal Affairs Bureau.

In identifying the overall role of prosecutors and their responsibility toward society, prosecutors are regarded as representatives of the public interest. They exercise their prosecutorial power for the purpose of maintaining law and order, based on the principle of strict fairness and impartiality, and with respect for suspects' human rights .

The police are primarily responsible for criminal investigations and carry out the initial investigations of more than 99 percent of criminal cases. Following their investigation they must refer cases to a public prosecutor together with relevant documents and evidence, even when the police believe that the evidence gathered is insufficient. The police have no power to finalize cases, except for minor offenses. Public prosecutors may also investigate cases themselves and often carry out supplementary investigations, that is, they interview victims and the main witnesses directly, and instruct the police to collect further evidence, if necessary. Moreover, public prosecutors may initiate and complete investigations without police assistance, and may do so in complicated cases, such as bribery or large-scale financial crimes involving politicians, senior government officials, or executives of large corporations.

THE SPECIAL INVESTIGATION DEPARTMENT OF THE PUBLIC PROSECUTORS OFFICE

In three major cities—Tokyo, Osaka, and Nagoya—the public prosecutors offices have special investigation departments where a considerable number of well trained and highly qualified public prosecutors and assistant officers are assigned to initiate investigations. The special investigation departments in the Tokyo and Osaka offices have a long history and have investigated many cases involving bribery, breach of trust, tax evasion, securities exchange violations, and the circumvention of laws such as those governing the prohibition of private monopolies and the maintenance of fair trade.

One of the best known cases involving a special investigation department may be the 1976 Lockheed scandal. In this case, the public prosecutors of the Special Investigation Department, Tokyo District Public Prosecutors Office, found that Lockheed Aircraft Corporation had paid millions of dollars (more than -500 million) to Japanese government officials through a Japanese agency, Marubeni Trading Corporation, to smooth the way for the sale of Lockheed's airplanes to a Japanese airline corporation, All Nippon Airways. Besides many executives of Marubeni and All Nippon Airways, the former prime minister, the former minister of transportation, and the former parliamentary vice-minister of transportation were arrested and prosecuted for giving and receiving bribes. The former prime minister was sentenced to four years imprisonment with forced labor. The Tokyo High Court rejected his appeal. He died while the case was in the Supreme Court, and so the case against him was dismissed in 1993.

Another noted scandal was the Recruit scandal. This was another large-scale corruption case that the same department handled in 1988. In this case, executives of Recruit Cosmos Corporation, a real estate company, and its mother company, Recruit Corporation, sold the rights to buy stocks that had been scheduled to be offered for public subscription and were sure to rise in value after that, to high-ranking government officials as bribes. These officials included the chief secretary to the prime minister, the vice minister of education, the vice-minister of labor, and the president of Japan Telephone and Telegram Corporation. All were arrested and prosecuted by public prosecutors. Some cases have been closed, while others are still being contested.

Yet another case involving the Tokyo Special Investigation Department was the Kyouwa scandal. This affair involved bribes amounting to approximately -80 million to Abe Fumio by Kyouwa, a firm that manufactures steel girders. When the scandal broke, Fumio was the secretary-general of the Liberal Democratic Party, the ruling party. Prior to that he had been head of the Hokkaido and Okinawa development agencies. In exchange for bribes he disclosed important government secrets to Kyouwa. Amid accusations of corruption, he resigned in December 1991. He was arrested in January 1992, and in May 1994 was sentenced to two years imprisonment with forced labor.

In 1994 the former minister of construction was arrested and indicted by the public prosecutor of the same department on the charge of receiving bribes in exchange for using his influence on behalf of the major construction corporation, Kajima. He was sentenced to 1 year and 6 months imprisonment with forced labor in 1997. The Tokyo High Court rejected his appeal and the case is still being contested in the Supreme Court.

SELF-INVESTIGATION BY SPECIAL INVESTIGATION DEPARTMENTS

The special investigation departments in the public prosecutors offices have special units for self-investigation where well-trained assistant officers keep an eye on department officials, in particular, by analyzing their bank account activity. When the department has reason to suspect an official of corruption, members of the special unit start tracing the official's bank accounts. Given the large number of financial institutions in Japan, this is no easy task; however, one approach is through the cooperation of credit card companies, which allow investigators to review credit card applications so that investigators can determine the bank accounts noted on the application. Once investigators have identified the accounts they track transactions to check for suspicious activity.

In some cases, a corrupt official will receive bribe money in the form of a check, for example, the vice-governor of Aichi prefecture received a bribe by check in the amount of some -20 million. In most cases, however, bribes are given in the form of cash, because cash is easier to conceal. Nevertheless, persistent and painstaking investigative work can also uncover cash bribes.

Let us consider the successful investigation of a bribery case by the special unit of the Osaka Public Prosecutors Office. The unit was investigating an official suspected of receiving bribes every month. The person giving the bribes paid them by using a false name at cash dispensers. Eventually the investigators managed to match up receipts from the cash dispensers from which the person suspected of giving the bribes was withdrawing the funds and the other automated teller machine where he was remitting the funds. This eventually allowed them to find the bank account of the person suspected of paying the bribes, as once they had the account number they could check the application form he had filled out to open the account to ascertain what name he had used.

ANALYSIS OF MATERIAL EVIDENCE

Japan's Code of Criminal Procedure requires that a judge must issue warrants for search and seizure and strictly restricts the extent of search and seizure. Under these regulations, material seized as evidence in relation to a particular case may lead to other cases. For example, during a tax evasion investigation, my office seized some receipts to use as evidence at trial; however, close examination of the receipts revealed that they had been doctored, and this led to the investigation being extended to a bribery offense in addition to tax evasion.

My office also investigated a case of bribery involving the mayor of the city of Wakayama—a city of some 400,000 people and a renowned tourist destination—and the former chairman of the Wakayama Municipal Assembly. The first clue was an item in a newspaper that reported that the Sennan City Agricultural Cooperative (SCAC) in Osaka had gone bankrupt. This is not usual for an agricultural cooperative. We knew that the SCAC had a bad reputation because of having too many bad loans on its books. Furthermore, Mr. X was one of the debtors, and we also knew him by reputation and had previously suspected him of giving bribes to local government officers and members of the local assembly. We therefore concluded that some breach of trust had occurred in the SCAC in relation to its loans and that Mr. X was probably involved, along with the head of the SCAC.

We started by asking for the cooperation of the Agricultural Cooperative Department in the Osaka prefectural government. This organization is responsible for supervising agricultural cooperatives in Osaka by periodically reviewing cooperatives' management and keeping track of their performance by means of reports and other documents. We received these various documents and reports and analyzed SCAC's loans. We also interviewed some SCAC staff. Eventually we determined that we had sufficient evidence to prosecute the head of SCAC and Mr. X for a breach of trust of -500 million. We arrested the head of SCAC, another SCAC staff member who was in charge of accounting, Mr. X, and a subordinate of Mr. X. A few days later they all confessed.

During the investigation we searched Mr. X's office and seized a certificate made by the Wakayama Land Development Agency. The certificate stated that the agency guaranteed to buy Mr. X's land. At first glance it was an ordinary certificate, but careful examination revealed some irregularities. One of these was the signature. Normally the head of issuing agency signs a certificate of this kind, but in this case the signature was that of a significantly lower-ranking official. Another irregularity was that the land was not as valuable as cited on the certificate. This led us to believe that Mr. X had bribed someone at the agency.

With this information in hand we interrogated Mr. X's subordinate. After an initial denial he confessed to giving a bribe of -5 million to Mr. Y, the former chairman of the Wakayama Municipal Assembly to pressure the head of the Wakayama Land Development Agency, also the mayor of Wakayama, to issue the certificate, because Mr. X and his subordinate thought that the certificate would significantly boost the value of the land.

After confronting Mr. X with his subordinate's confession, Mr. X also eventually confessed to giving the - 5 million bribe to Mr. Y. Thus we eventually also obtained a confession from Mr. Y. However, at this stage, we could not arrest the mayor of Wakayama, because he had ordered a subordinate to make the certificate and sign it, and we had insufficient evidence to prove that the mayor had committed a crime. We did, however, have sufficient grounds to search the mayor's office. We examined his daily work records and found a reference to a meeting between his subordinate, Mr. Z, early one weekend morning in his office, which was unusual. We had also learned from Mr. Y about a scheme whereby parents could get their children employed at the Wakayama Administrative Office by giving the mayor -1 million. An investigation of Mr. Z found that his daughter had gained entry to the office even though she had performed worse on the entrance examination than other candidates who had not been employed by the office.

Following further investigation we arrested the mayor, his secretary, and Mr. Z. We also interviewed Mr. Z's wife, who was familiar with the whole story. They all confessed to the recruitment scheme and were indicted. The arrest and indictment of a mayor of a city of this size is rare and caused quite a sensation. At trial, all the defendants admitted their guilt and received appropriate sentences.

This case underscores the importance of analyzing material evidence. If we had not noticed the irregularities in the certificate or found the reference to a meeting between the mayor and Mr. Z, we would not have found the second crime, the recruitment scheme.

NEED FOR NEW INVESTIGATIVE TOOLS

In the case of the mayor of Wakayama, we fortunately obtained confessions from all the suspects. Recently, however, investigations have tended to become more difficult. We should therefore consider introducing new investigative techniques, such as granting immunity in exchange for information. In terms of combating transnational organized crime, paragraph 3 of Article 23 of the United Nations Convention against Transnational Organized Crime states that each nation shall consider granting immunity from prosecution. I believe that an immunity system is necessary for the investigation of both corruption cases as well as transnational organized crime.

Japan currently does not have an immunity system, which has led to a number of problems as evidenced by the Lockheed scandal. As mentioned earlier, the former prime minister died while the case was in the Supreme Court, and the case was dismissed without any judgments being handed down. Yet the former chairman of Marubeni Trading was indicted for giving a -500 million bribe to the former prime minister. The Supreme Court dismissed the chairman's appeal and pronounced him guilty. However, this judgment came as a surprise to public prosecutors and judges, because the Supreme Court had denied the admissibility of the depositions of Archibald Kotchian, former chairman of Lockheed, and John Clatter, former director of Lockheed's office in Japan.

The scandal first became evident with testimony given by Kotchian and Clatter in the United States. A public prosecutor from the Tokyo District Public Prosecutors Office asked a Tokyo District Court judge to seek permission to obtain depositions from Kotchian and Clatter. Following the prosecutor's request to the court, the prosecutor-general issued a written declaration that he had instructed the chief prosecutor of the Tokyo District Public Prosecutors Office not to prosecute Kotchian, Clatter, and others (based on Article 248 of the Code of Criminal Procedure) even if it turned out that their actions had contravened Japanese law.

Upon receiving the request, the U.S. District Court for the Central District of California, which had jurisdiction over the case, appointed a commissioner to preside over the taking of depositions. However, both Kotchian and Clatter refused to testify, questioning the legality of their immunity in Japan and whether it would actually hold up in court. Consequently, the U.S. judge ordered the depositions to be taken but not to be provided to the Japanese court until he had received confirmation from the Supreme Court of Japan that clearly stated that the witnesses would not be prosecuted in Japan. On receipt of such a guarantee, the depositions were provided to Japanese prosecutors.

As noted earlier, the Supreme Court of Japan consequently denied the admissibility of the depositions on the grounds that while the Constitution cannot be construed as rejecting the concept of immunity, the Code of Criminal Procedure has no such provisions. While criminal immunity serves practical purposes, it also benefits those involved in a crime and affects criminal procedure. Therefore the decision on whether or not to adopt the system should consider whether circumstances warrant the introduction of such a system, whether it is compatible with the notion of a fair trial, and whether the public will perceive it to be fair. If the system is to be adopted, provisions regarding its use would have to be drafted. As the Criminal Code does not contain such provisions, the implication is that criminal immunity cannot be used, and therefore testimony obtained in exchange for criminal immunity is inadmissible. Therefore, excluding the depositions in the Lockheed case was appropriate under the circumstances.

This judgment revealed the limitations of the interpretation of Japanese legislation. Yet despite the passage of six years since the Lockheed judgment, consensus about the introduction of immunity has not been reached. I believe that we will have an opportunity to revisit this issue when Japan enacts new laws as part of its ratification of the United Nations Convention against Transnational Organized Crime.

CONCLUSION

Preventing corruption is important, yet it poses many difficulties. I hope that when the United Nations reviews this issue, as it is scheduled to do in 2002, that this will result in new guidelines or a new convention. Japan should consider enacting new laws or revising existing laws against corruption and introducing new investigative techniques to improve the investigation and prosecution of bribery cases.

Chapter 12

Conditions for Effective Reform

■ **Gerald A. Sumida**

On 31 May 2001 the 143 countries taking part in the Second Global Forum on Fighting Corruption and Safeguarding Integrity stated in their Final Declaration that:

> We are all deeply concerned about the spread of corruption, which is a virus capable of crippling government, discrediting public institutions and private corporations and having a devastating impact on the human rights of populations, and thus undermining society and its development, affecting in particular the poor.[1]

This succinct, but compelling, statement crystallizes the destructive impacts of corruption in general, and its corrosive and debilitating effects on the development process and on developing societies in particular.

For multilateral development financial institutions such as the ADB, an effective fight against corruption in the Asia-Pacific region is of paramount importance. The ADB and its developing member countries work in close partnership to design and implement development projects and initiatives aimed at reducing the region's widespread poverty and fostering economic growth and social development with the objectives of enhancing the quality of life and promoting human dignity. Corruption is the cancer that insinuates itself into the living fabric of society to cripple it and, if left unchecked, to destroy society's will, aspirations, and efforts to achieve sustainable economic growth and social development. Hence, fighting corruption is necessarily a part of the ADB's development agenda.[2]

---

[1] The Second Global Forum was held in The Hague during 28-31 May 2001. It was cosponsored by the Netherlands and the United States and assisted by an organizing committee comprising representatives of several countries and international organizations. It cooperated closely with the International Anti-Corruption Conference, which held its 10th annual meeting in Prague in October 2001. Both conferences plan to convene in Seoul in 2003.

[2] This has been articulated in the ADB's official policies on Governance: Sound Development

In this conference we are focusing on specific approaches to combating corruption effectively, many of which are stated in the Action Plan that has emerged from prior conferences as a working document and could become a foundation for regional action. It is within this context that the role of the judiciary in improving the investigation and prosecution of bribery in particular is of special interest.

INTERNATIONAL LEGISLATION TO COMBAT BRIBERY

Bribery has become a high priority target in the fight against corruption, largely because of the global expansion of international trade, commerce, and investment. This expansion has been led by multinational business enterprises, later supplemented by global investment funds, generally based in North America and Europe, and by increasing flows of bilateral and multilateral development assistance to the developing countries (among the vast literature on this subject see, in particular, Martin 1999; Rose-Ackerman 1999). In its purest essence, "Bribery is a breach of people's trust" (Martin 1999, p. 12). We know that bribery diminishes, if not eliminates, competition; creates and exacerbates inefficiencies; and ultimately increases costs for countries and their consumers, especially the poor. Countries with high levels of corruption have poorer quality and amounts of public investment, which in turn is associated with lower private investment, and ultimately leads to lower economic growth rates (see Everhart and Sumlinski 2001).

The pioneering international initiative against bribery is the OECD Convention on Combating Bribery of Foreign Public Officials in International Business Transactions (the OECD Convention), which entered into force on 15 February 1999 and has been signed by all 30 OECD member countries and 5 nonmember countries. It requires that each government establish that it is a criminal offense under its law

> for any person intentionally to offer, promise or give any undue pecuniary or other advantage, whether directly or though intermediaries, to a foreign public official, for that official or for a third party, in order that the official act or refrain from acting in relation to the performance of official duties, in order to obtain or retain business or other improper advantage in the conduct of international business.

Management (1995) and Anti-Corruption (1998) and its extensive projects and technical assistance in these areas.

Furthermore, each government must also establish as criminal offenses complicity in (including incitement and aiding and abetting) or authorization of an act of bribery of a foreign official, as well as the attempt and a conspiracy to bribe a public official of its own government. Such offenses are to be punishable by "effective, proportionate and dissuasive criminal penalties." The OECD Convention also requires each government to take measures regarding maintaining accurate records, disclosing financial statements, providing mutual legal assistance to other signatories, cooperating in extradition and surveillance, and monitoring compliance.[3] In addition, certain OECD recommendations call upon OECD members to end the practice of allowing bribe payments made to foreign officials to be tax deductible.

The OECD Convention prohibits only the offering or paying of bribes, but not the soliciting or taking of bribes. In contrast, the Inter-American Convention against Corruption (the OAS Convention) requires that governments establish as criminal offenses under their laws both the solicitation or acceptance, directly or indirectly, of a bribe by a public official, as well as the offering or granting, directly or indirectly, of a bribe to a public official. The OAS Convention also provides for the adoption of standards of conduct, the criminalization of unexplained increases in wealth while in public office and of illicit enrichment, the improper use of classified or confidential information obtained during the performance of public functions, and other measures similar to those in the OECD Convention. The OAS Convention was signed by 29 countries and entered into force on 6 March 1997.

These intergovernmental efforts to combat bribery in international business transactions are supplemented by the activities of international nongovernment organizations. For example, Transparency International periodically issues its Corruption Perceptions Index, which rates countries based on perceptions of the degree of corruption as seen by business people, risk analysts, and the general public. In 1999 Transparency International published its Bribe Payers Index, which rates 19 leading exporting countries based on perceptions of each country's willingness to pay bribes abroad.[4]

---

[3] The United States had previously enacted the Foreign Corrupt Practices Act, signed into law in 1977, which prohibits paying bribes to foreign officials and imposes rigorous record keeping and accounting requirements on US companies and their overseas subsidiaries to ensure that bribes cannot be hidden. No other country had followed the lead of the United States until the OECD Convention was signed.

[4] See http://www.transparency.org/documents cip/1999/bps.html. Among the five countries rated as having the greatest willingness to pay bribes abroad were four Asian countries (in descending order): Malaysia; Taipei,China; Republic of Korea, and PRC.

This is reinforced by actions such as the International Chamber of Commerce's adoption in 1996 of its Rules and Recommendations on Extortion and Bribery in International Business Transactions, which prohibit both demanding and accepting a bribe.[5]

NATIONAL LEGISLATION TO COMBAT BRIBERY

A review of how we might combat bribery at the national and subnational levels in the Asia-Pacific region reveals four basic conditions that have profound implications for how we should craft and implement strategies to combat corruption in general, and bribery in particular, namely:

- In many cases, laws prohibiting corrupt acts, including bribery, are on the books; however, tightening up and updating these laws may be necessary, along with supplementing them with additional useful laws, such as freedom of information laws and similar measures aimed at achieving greater transparency and accountability.
- In most cases, what is clearly and glaringly absent is the prompt, effective, systematic, and non-discriminatory enforcement of these laws. Indeed, often there is simply no enforcement.
- In most cases, effective enforcement is lacking because the capacity to enforce these laws is extremely weak. That is, countries lack sufficient trained, professionally-oriented, adequately compensated, properly equipped, visibly and continuously supported, publicly respected men and women. Such people are needed to understand, publicize, counsel about, engender respect for, enforce, investigate, prosecute accused persons under, and vindicate these laws. In addition, they must often perform these duties in the face of ignorance of these laws; resistance to enforcement efforts; threats to their own and their families' safety; and the intangible, but powerful, force of social traditions and attitudes that condone, if not actually encourage, such practices.
- In most cases, effective enforcement faces institutional and operational obstacles, if not outright barriers, because there is no clear separation between and among the judicial system, the police administration, the investigative and prosecutorial administration, and other parts of the governmental structure involved in law enforcement and the administration of justice. Where institutional separation, especially of the judiciary from the rest of the system of justice administration, is weak or blurred, and where the judiciary and judicial administration

---

[5] See http://www.iccwbo.org/home/statements_rules/rules/1996/1996/briberydoc.asp.

are weak, then even the best laws will remain weakly enforced, if enforced at all.

ROLE OF THE JUDICIARY

We must therefore recognize that improving techniques and approaches for investigating and prosecuting bribery and other forms of corruption will not work in isolation from the public institutions and attitudes that underlie an effective judiciary and judicial system and, more broadly, a system based on the rule of law. From this perspective, it is useful to review the roles and functions of the judiciary as a fundamental element of the societal order. Overall the judiciary has five dimensions and specific missions (see Dator 2001; Sugimoto and Yasutomi 1981):

- As a *branch of government* the judiciary's mission is to uphold the constitution and the government thereby created, the rights and liberties that the constitution guarantees, and the policies and principles that it embodies.
- As a *dispute resolution forum* the judiciary's mission is to ensure that the public has access to the highest standard of justice attainable under the country's system of government by assuring the equitable and expeditious resolution of all cases and controversies properly brought before the courts, and by facilitating alternative forms of dispute resolution to supplement the formal court system.
- As a *public agency* the judiciary's mission is to provide for, promote, and ensure effective, economical, and efficient use of public resources in the administration of the judicial system.
- As a *subsystem of the country's legal system* the judiciary's mission is to promote effective and expeditious administration of justice by the various other elements of the legal system.
- As an *institution of a changing society* the judiciary's mission is to anticipate and respond to society's changing judicial needs.

From this perspective, a judiciary that embodies these institutional dimensions and missions is an institution based on, and in turn an essential part of, the society's legal order, the basis of which is the rule of law. It is not only a branch of the government and a public body, but it is the central, though not exclusive, forum for the resolution of the society's legally-based disputes. As part of the society, it must not only be responsive to change as the society as a whole changes, but it must also be acutely aware of its proper role in influencing and shaping the future of the society of which it is part.

The effectiveness of the judiciary and the judicial system ultimately depends on the existence of the rule of law and the sound and efficient operation of the core legal institutions and the supporting civil society institutions and processes. Indeed, these are fundamental prerequisites for an effective economic, social, and political order essential for a modern society in our increasingly interdependent world. The institution of the judiciary—the formal court adjudicatory system—lies at the heart of a society's legal order. Without an effective, functioning, and independent judicial system the results for society are inevitable and predictable: uncertainty will pervade society; the efficient conduct of business and economic affairs will face oppressive burdens; social integration and development will be strongly resisted; and widespread injustice and deprivation of the rights of ordinary citizens, especially the poor, women, and children, will be likely.

Finally, the effectiveness of a judiciary also depends on the concurrent development of other institutions and attitudes within the broader society that support, as well as rely upon, a strong, capable, and independent judiciary. However, the need to ensure that the judiciary itself is an effectively functioning institution is paramount.

JUDICIAL REFORMS

In considering the most effective approaches and strategies for combating bribery, three interrelated areas of reform are crucial. The first targets the judiciary as the key institution in fighting corruption, the second comprises specific anti-corruption and anti-bribery measures, and the third relates to complementary institutional reforms.

When considering initiatives that will strengthen the institutional capabilities of the judiciary, reformers should keep in mind several considerations that can determine whether or not such initiatives are ultimately successful. These considerations include the following:

- Any effort at comprehensive judicial reform falls within a much broader societal context that centers on strengthening the rule of law in general, including public attitudes toward the rule of law and the legal order, and that recognizes the fundamental need to provide ordinary citizens with access to justice and the confidence that the judiciary will provide impartial, prompt, and clear results.
- Any judicial reform effort must have the government's full commitment and must be led by the highest judicial officials, in particular, the chief

justice of the supreme court. Without this firm support and vigorous leadership the needed changes, especially in institutional attitudes and culture within the judicial institutions, will be unsustainable.

- The reform effort will be a long-term, multiyear program and must be effectively planned, staffed, funded, monitored, and supported during that entire period. Changing the attitudes and the culture of court and judiciary personnel is fundamental, as is providing them with the necessary material resources, knowledge, and skills to make the reforms work on a sustainable basis. This takes time and persistent efforts, and must be clearly anticipated. Quick fixes or one-shot reform efforts will inevitably prove to be unsustainable.

- Other public institutions and agencies also influence the fulfillment and realization of citizens' legal entitlements and must similarly be brought into the reform effort. They include the police administration, the prosecutors' and defense offices, and legal aid services. Ultimately, the success of any judicial reform efforts, including strengthening the independence of the judiciary, will be affected by how these other public institutions and agencies are reformed.

- The public must accept and support any reform effort and perceive it as credible. Sources of support from citizens include established bodies, such as bar, legal, and other professional associations; law, business, and other professional schools; chambers of commerce and other business organizations; and grassroots citizen groups and organizations.

The range of possible judicial reforms is limited only by imagination, but include the following, which must be based on the specific needs of each society:

- Improve policymaking in the judicial sector, possibly by establishing a national law commission. This commission would deal systematically with policy issues involving the judicial system, including policies related to the training of judges and court administration personnel, funding, human resource development, and standards of conduct and discipline.

- Strengthen judicial independence, including completely separating the judiciary from the executive branch of government and ensuring adequate funding and independence in staffing for the judiciary.

- Ensure the efficient and cost-effective administration of justice, including improving case management, reducing court congestion, developing bench books and trial practice manuals, establishing a judicial training academy for judges and other court personnel, setting up small causes or small claims courts, initiating court-annexed arbitration and mediation systems, and computerizing the court system (including links to the police and prison systems).

- Improve the general public's knowledge of their legal rights to access to the courts, including publishing laws in local languages, developing public information and awareness programs, initiating law review programs, and adopting freedom of information and consumer protection laws.
- Improve judicial governance, including employing professional judiciary administration managers, establishing ombudsman positions, developing a human resources development strategy, and instituting systems to hold judges accountable.
- Improve human resource development, including developing a judiciary-wide human resources development strategy, reviewing and adopting new personnel policies and procedures as needed, developing the capacity to provide in-service training to the judiciary, and developing training and educational liaisons with academic and private sector sources.

ANTI-BRIBERY MEASURES

Improving the investigation and prosecution of bribery can be pursued through several specific courses of action, a number of which are already incorporated in the Action Plan as follows (see also the annex to the Final Declaration of the Second Global Forum for compilations of measures for combating bribery and corruption; Bhargava and Bolongaita 2001 for an assessment of various anti-corruption instruments; Jayawickrama 1998):

- Ensure the adoption of well-drafted and clearly stated legislation that covers the following critical matters and provides for strong and appropriately dissuasive minimum sanctions for violations:

  - A law that criminalizes soliciting, receiving, offering, and paying bribes; money laundering; and similar crimes and that provides dissuasive sanctions. This may require a special evidentiary provision containing a rebuttable presumption that public officials who have more money or property that what they could legitimately have earned or who maintain a standard of living beyond what is commensurate with their official emoluments be deemed to have acquired such money, property, or other wealth through corruption.
  - A law that enables tracing, seizing, freezing, and forfeiture of illicit earnings from corruption, which also stipulates that any contract,

license, or approval obtained through this means will be void and unenforceable and the person convicted of corruption will be disqualified from responding to public contract tenders.

- A law that requires the regular and periodic declaration of assets, income, and liabilities by decisionmakers and public officials who hold positions where they interact with the public and are well placed to extract bribes, together with an independent monitoring and enforcement agency that regularly reviews such declarations.
- A law that identifies and prevents or resolves conflicts of interest, especially those involving public officials' private and public interests.
- A law that provides a strong recovery mechanism under civil law (as distinct from criminal law) to govern the recovery of illicitly acquired assets from family members, friends, acquaintances, and associates of persons convicted of corruption. Civil court judgments are usually more readily enforceable in foreign jurisdictions to which assets may have been moved.

- Ensure that no existing laws can be used to frustrate the operation of anti-bribery laws, such as criminal and civil defamation laws that could be used against those alleging corruption and those covering corruption in the media, or that any such laws are amended to preclude their use to frustrate the prosecution of corruption.
- Ensure that laws and appropriate implementing regulations are adopted and promulgated to provide for effective, prompt, and thorough investigation and prosecution of all those accused of bribery offenses by competent authorities.
- Strengthen the investigative and prosecutorial capacities of pertinent public agencies by providing sufficient funding, personnel, training, equipment, recruitment and retention programs, and other resources; developing and expanding communications and operational relationships with other government departments and agencies involved in judicial and law enforcement; and developing, promulgating, and enforcing standards of performance and integrity, including investigative and disciplinary mechanisms, to institutionalize professionalism and integrity.
- Strengthen and enhance bilateral and multilateral cooperation in carrying out investigations and other legal proceedings to further information and evidence exchange, extradition, cooperative search and seizure, and prompt repatriation of forfeitable assets; training personnel and participating in exchange programs; and engaging in research and development on how to deal effectively with transnational criminal activities involving corruption, in particular bribery.

The broader institutional structure through which anti-corruption, including anti-bribery, laws are enforced and implemented is also critically important to complement the appropriate laws. The successful enforcement of anti-corruption legislation can be significantly enhanced by an institutional framework that includes the following:

- Establish an independent commission against corruption charged with implementing the anti-corruption legislation. This commission must be backed by committed political support at the highest levels of government; be politically and operationally independent and have that independence sustained by public pressure; possess adequate powers to obtain evidence and question witnesses; have leadership that is publicly perceived as being of the highest integrity and personnel of the highest professional ability; and be publicly accountable, preferably to the legislative body.
- Ensure the existence of an independent prosecuting agency, not subject to any external agency, political or otherwise, that is separate from the police and court systems, and that has the authority to decide whether or not to institute criminal proceedings.
- Ensure the existence of an independent, accountable, transparent, and professional police force free from political interference. This may include setting up public safety or police commissions to ensure civilian control and institutionalize the accountability of the police force and gender and human rights awareness within the police system and establishing liaison committees to improve relations between the police and the public.
- Create an independent authority to investigate complaints against the police.
- Create the post of auditor-general responsible for auditing government income and expenditure, including ensuring that the executive complies with the legislature as expressed through parliamentary appropriations, promoting efficiency and cost-effectiveness in government operations, and preventing corruption through the development of financial and auditing procedures designed to reduce the incidence of corruption and increase the likelihood of its detection. Ideally, this office should be constitutionally established and protected.
- Create the post of ombudsman, who will receive and investigate allegations of maladministration ranging from incompetence and delays to bribery and corruption. This should be an independent officer to whom citizens have direct access, with appropriate measures to ensure confidentiality, and whose independence and security are constitutionally protected.

Furthermore, corruption and bribery can be curbed by limiting situations in which they can occur and by reducing the benefits to both recipient and payer, that is, by rendering both more vulnerable to detection and sanctions. An anti-corruption strategy should therefore include the following:

- Define the discretionary element in decisionmaking narrowly, especially concerning procedures for government agencies charged with granting approvals, licenses, and permits and undertaking public procurement.
- Institute Internet- and electronically-based permitting and public procurement systems, which can make these otherwise often complicated and hidden processes public and accessible, and also simplify them, thereby removing their vulnerability to corruption.
- Revise, redesign, and repeal, where appropriate or desirable, the mass of rules, regulations, procedures, and formalities, leaving only those that are necessary for conducting required operations. Ensure that those rules, regulations, and procedures that remain in effect are clear, plainly understandable by ordinary citizens, and accessible.
- Ensure the adoption of legislation and appropriate regulations, as well as the ability to enforce government agency compliance, that provide for greater disclosure of information and transparency in government operations, especially public procurement and investment matters, by:
  - Publishing budgets and other routine information promptly and predictably
  - Passing a freedom of information act that provides a simple procedure allowing citizens to request and obtain government documents
  - Publishing and disseminating laws, regulations, and agency and judicial decisions promptly upon their adoption or issuance and in a manner that is accessible to the public
  - Having public agencies use the Internet to provide information about the agencies and their operations and decisions
  - Mandating annual disclosure by public officials and their families, including members of the judiciary, of their assets and requiring them to explain any unusual increases in such assets that cannot be accounted for by their public remuneration
  - Passing a whistle-blower protection act, extended to those within the government and the media, to provide protection from retribution for those who provide information about corruption.
- Undertake administrative reforms that minimize opportunities for corrupt practices.
- Demystify government by explaining government decisionmaking

processes by, for example, publishing tax collectors' and other handbooks and placing the onus on civil servants to justify why they are withholding access to documents.

- Institute a meritocratic civil service, whereby civil servants are recruited on the basis of merit, adequately remunerated, and assured of career advancement solely on the basis of merit.

In addition to these specific approaches, the business community and civil society, including professional and trade associations, nongovernment organizations, academic institutions, and the public at large, must be integrally enlisted in a continuing campaign against corruption. This involves programs of public awareness and support for the anti-corruption efforts of public authorities engaged in enforcing, investigating, and prosecuting bribery and corruption.

CONCLUSIONS

The caveat to all these approaches and specific techniques to combat corruption is that the highest levels of government must be strongly committed to pursing anti-bribery and anti-corruption strategies and initiatives vigorously and persistently. That commitment must be visible, forceful, and convincing. It must also enlist the legislative and judicial branches of government, the business community, and civil society as strong and equally committed parties. Without this commitment and increasingly widespread public support, any anti-corruption strategy and program will fail.

As the region's developing countries seek to continue their national programs of economic and social development, the rule of law is clearly fundamental to this process. The rule of law is not to control or to direct a society, but to provide the basic foundation and order for effective, efficient, and just operations of the many different facets of the society's governance system and to safeguard the basic rights and entitlements, and concomitant civic duties and responsibilities, of all citizens. It involves written stipulations and guarantees in constitutions, laws, and regulations. It also involves a culture infused by widespread attitudes and expectations that all citizens can confidently rely on the legal system. Fundamental to all this, and especially to the public's confidence in this legal order, is the judicial system.

Therefore our focus on the role of the judiciary in combating bribery and corruption is appropriate. Indeed, as history clearly shows, a strong, independent, professional, efficient, and respected judiciary is pivotal to the survival of human rights and human dignity in society. As a partner in the fight against bribery and corruption and in efforts to promote good governance, the ADB will continue to support the strengthening of judicial institutions and the rule of law in the Asia-Pacific region.

REFERENCES

Bhargava, Vinay K., and Emil P. Bolongaita, Jr. 2001. Making National Anti-Corruption Policies and Programs More Effective: An Analytical Framework. Draft.

Dator, Jim. 2001. Maintaining Confidence in Our Legal Institutions: Past Practices/Future Challenges. Paper delivered at the 17th LawAsia Biennial Conference and 9th Conference of Chief Justices of Asia and the Pacific, 4-8 October, Christchurch, New Zealand.

Everhart, Stephen S., and Mariusz A. Sumlinski. 2001. *Trends in Private Investment in Developing Countries: Statistics for 1970-2000 and the Impact on Private Investment of Corruption and the Quality of Public Investment.* Discussion Paper no. 44. Washington, DC: International Finance Corporation.

Jayawickrama, Nihal. 1998. Combating Corruption in Asia: Legal and Institutional Reform. Background paper for the conference on Integrity in Governance in Asia, 29 June-1 July, Bangkok, Thailand.

Martin, A. Timothy. 1999. The Development of International Bribery Law. *Natural Resources and Environment* (fall).

Rose-Ackerman, Susan. 1999. *Corruption and Government: Causes, Consequences, and Reform.* Cambridge, UK: Cambridge University Press.

Sugimoto, Gregory, and Wayne Yasutomi. 1981. The Conceptual Framework of the Judiciary. In *Comprehensive Planning in the Hawaii Judiciary.* Honolulu, Hawaii: Hawaii State Judiciary.

PART III

**Strengthening Civic Participation
in the Fight Against Corruption**

F. Interaction Between Governments and
   Nongovernment Organizations
G. Society in Action Against Corruption

F. Interaction Between Governments and Nongovernment Organizations

Chapter 13

Interaction between the Government of the Kyrgyz Republic and Local Nongovernment Organizations to Foster Good Governance

■ **Tolondu Toichubaev**

Following independence, the Kyrgyz Republic has embarked on a number of political and economic reforms aimed at socioeconomic development, poverty reduction, and an enhanced role for civil society.

As frequently stressed by the government and donor organizations, an important component of any national policy aimed at poverty reduction is combating corruption. The growing body of research in the field of good governance reveals a correlation between poverty and corruption. Even though corruption occurs in every country, it is most destructive and most prevalent in those countries that can least afford it. Those governments most passionate about combating corruption are usually those that have assumed power following the overthrow of a previous regime.

Important factors in combating corruption are the existence of both the political will and the corresponding public will to fight it. The need for a long-term and sustainable approach to fighting corruption is essential, and requires public support if it is to be achieved. One way to engender public support for an anti-corruption program is to involve civil society.

Thus the success of any anti-corruption campaign ultimately depends on society's willingness to support it, which also involves changing public perceptions of what is culturally acceptable. Therefore modifying corrupt behavior by public servants requires modifying the perceptions and values of the society in which they live. One of the best ways to bring the people into the reform process is to include one important group of stakeholders, namely, civil society organizations.

In relation to anti-corruption, NGOs should focus on the following three key activities:

- Creating public awareness about corruption and the need to control it
- Formulating action plans to fight corruption and influencing governments to adopt them
- Monitoring governments' actions and decisions that might entail corruption or could reduce corruption.

CSOs are often much more effective than governments in monitoring and promoting the governance reform process. In addition, the involvement of CSOs gives more credibility to the fight against corruption. Citizens generally have a hard time believing that a systematically corrupt government is going to combat corruption. The government of Kazakhstan came to realize this following the June 1999 anti-corruption conference in Astana, Kazakhstan (Bowser-2001). Before the conference the government had not included CSOs in the National Anti-Corruption Committee. Following the presentations by NGOs and the speeches by representatives of the international donor community during the conference, the government invited several NGOs to join this policy group. The danger for CSOs involved in anti-corruption activities is that they may be used as "fig leaves" to mask political interests. In addition, NGOs are not above using the corruption issue as a means of government opposition.

Another important factor in increasing the public will for anti-corruption initiatives is overcoming public cynicism. The public perception in the former Soviet Union countries is that corruption is an integral part of public life and cannot be eliminated. Any anti-corruption efforts will be viewed through this prism and an excellent public information campaign must therefore accompany any anti-corruption program. One aspect of this that governments wishing to combat corruption often ignore is the need for a free and active press that can act as a watchdog in relation to corruption matters.

According to a survey carried out in the Kyrgyz Republic by the Center for Public Opinion Studies and Forecasting, 24 percent of the population and 47 percent of business people consider the press, television, and radio as the government's main ally in the fight against corruption (table 13.1). The table also shows that NGOs are still not recognized as a strong ally in combating corruption.

| Table 13.1.
Whom Should the Authorities Use as Allies in the Fight against
Bribery and Corruption ||||
| Potential allies | Percentage of respondents ||
	Public	Business people
Law enforcement bodies	27.1	11.1
Press, television, and radio	24.1	47.1
Don't know	13.1	15.0
Political parties	12.0	4.1
Ordinary citizens	8.1	8.0
NGOs	7.1	5.1
Entrepreneurs	4.1	6.0
Religious bodies	3.0	0.3
Other	1.0	3.0
Trade unions	0.4	0.3

Source: Ilibezova and others (2000).

While civil society activism can help pressure governments to answer to the public, civil society is most effective when the government treats it as an ally rather than an enemy. In Slovakia, for example, a Slovak NGO was entrusted with preparing the first draft of the national program for the fight against corruption and has regularly been invited to monitor procurements and other state decisions—a testimony to the strength of the partnership between the current government and civil society.

Constructive state policy toward civil society enhances the role that civil society can play and its contribution. An example of productive cooperation between the government and civil society in the Kyrgyz Republic was the recent approval of the Comprehensive Development Framework (CDF) and the National Strategy for Poverty Reduction (NSPR). The objective of the CDF is to develop a strategy for formulating a long-term plan for 2010. Major work initiated by the government under the World Bank-financed Plan of Participation of Civil Society in Implementation of the CDF and NSPR Project was carried out with the active participation of civil society support centers and the Counterpart Consortium during 2000-2001. As a result of this initiative, NGOs submitted more than 500 recommendations and proposals on the CDF. Over 400 leaders and activists from 300 nonprofit organizations took part in roundtable meetings organized by civil society support centers and the Counterpart Consortium. More than 1,000 people representing local communities, the private sector, state authorities, political parties, and the mass media were involved in 2001.

Participants at the roundtable meetings representing seven *oblasts* made many constructive recommendations to the Plan of Participation. The main purpose of drafting the plan was to stipulate the participation (projects, programs, initiatives, actions, and so on) that could be implemented under the CDF and NSPR in the future.

Active support of the civil society support centers and other stakeholders ensured the development of a CDF/NSPR stakeholder map (database) with key information about stakeholders (names of organizations, main activities, available resources and facilities, target groups, addresses).

The involvement of civil society in this project expanded its geographical coverage and drew in new participants. For the first time public organizations had the opportunity to participate in the development of a strategic document and rural noncommercial organizations and communities could take part in the discussions. Many roundtables attracted 30 to 40 participants rather than the projected 20, underscoring civil society's interest in participating in the drafting of the CDF and NSPR.

NGOs' participation in the development of the overall national strategy does not preclude their involvement in attempting to assure good governance. At the legislative level representatives of NGOs, public associations, and political parties are involved in parliamentary sessions on various social issues. They also examine new legislation. In particular, for the first time in the history of Central Asia women's NGOs reviewed all Kyrgyz legislation with respect to gender and prepared drafts of several laws especially relevant to women.

The Kyrgyz Republic has also legally adopted the use of public observers for elections. During the last election civil society representatives also realized their right to participate officially in the work of district election commissions and of the Central Election Commission.

At the local level civil society representatives were given an opportunity to take part in public hearings on local budgets, which were held in a number of *raions.*

At the executive level a considerable number of NGOs and other civil groups are involved in various national programs as well as in the conventions on children's rights and on the abolition of discrimination against women and in monitoring implementation of the Human Rights Declaration. NGOs play an active role in training civil servants in such areas as gender sensitivity and new ways to work with victims of violence. An example of a partnership between the authorities and civil society is the involvement of the Congress of Local Communities in the United Nations Development Programme's Decentralization Program. The program's aim is to create and develop opportunities for civil society participation in making decisions that directly influence people's lives.

NGOs are also involved at the judicial level, for example, by conducting independent monitoring the implementation of legislation.

Nevertheless, civil society involvement in good governance still faces a number of problems. For instance, NGOs themselves may be perpetrators of corruption as demonstrated by the experience of the former Soviet Union. In a number of countries NGOs have sprung up simply to tap into the assistance dollars that external donors have been prepared to provide to organizations to help strengthen civil society. Moves are starting to explore ways to ensure that NGOs are more transparent and accountable. Just like official institutions, NGOs cannot be taken at face value and need to be monitored for transparency.

According a report by the European Bank for Reconstruction and Development (ECA External Advisory Board 2000) the level of corruption, both administrative corruption and state capture, in the Kyrgyz Republic is one of the highest among the countries in transition and in the world (figures

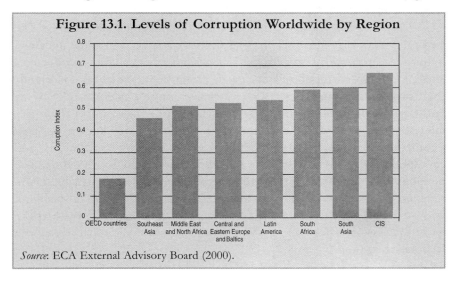

Figure 13.1. Levels of Corruption Worldwide by Region

Source: ECA External Advisory Board (2000).

13.1 and 13.2). According to a summary index developed from a weighted average of 12 of the most widely known cross-country corruption indexes with data from 1996-1999, the level of corruption in the countries of the Commonwealth of Independent States (CIS) exceeds that in South Asia and southern Africa.

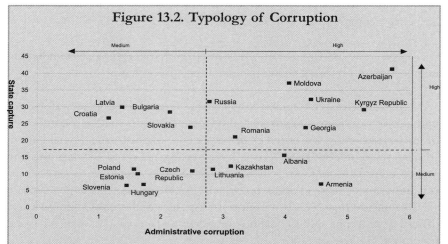

Figure 13.2. Typology of Corruption

Note: Administrative corruption is measured as the average firm's expenditure on administrative corruption as a share of its annual revenue in each country. The index of state capture for each country is created by taking the average of the share of firms that report a significant impact on their business from each of the various forms of state capture.

Source: European Bank for Reconstruction and Development.

As the figures show, the fight against corruption still has far to go. The Central Asian Corporate Technologies Center came up with some initiatives in this area. In cooperation with the Talas *oblast* farmers union it conducted a small, local anti-corruption campaign to create public awareness. Currently the Corporate Technologies Center is implementing a national pilot of an anti-corruption project known as "Corporate Conversation." This is a television program on which some of the country's well-known business people are interviewed about national goals, ideology, education, and corruption. The interviewees have indicated that for the Kyrgyz Republic's development corruption is a much more significant problem than high taxation rates, complicated licensing procedures, inadequate numbers of inspections, and so on. To promote further dialogue an Internet site—http://www.tv.ctc.kg—has been set up where all those interested can participate in a web-based forum.

Civil society believes that with active involvement of civil society it will gradually alleviate the problem of corruption and further enforce good governance.

REFERENCES

Bowser, Donald. 2001. Anti-Corruption Best Practices. Report prepared for the government of the Kyrgyz Republic.

ECA External Advisory Board on Governance. 2000. Anticorruption in Transition: Confronting the Challenge of State Capture. Draft summary report.

Ilibezova, E., L. Ilibezova, N. Asanbaev, and G. Musokojaeva. 2000. *Corruption in Kyrgyzstan*. Bishkek, Kyrgyz Republic: Center for Public Opinion Studies and Forecasting.

Chapter 14

Government — Nongovernment Organization Interaction in Drafting the Republic of Korea's Anti-Corruption Law

■ **Tae-Ho Lee**

Now more than ever, Koreans are concerned about the problem of corruption and ways to deal with it. Recently the government of the Republic of Korea introduced new laws and regulations against corruption and money laundering. This change was accelerated by a series of corruption scandals and the subsequent 1997 national financial crisis, and was clearly initiated as a result of a grassroots effort by civil society. Since 1996 the legislative campaign by the People's Solidarity for Participatory Democracy (PSPD) and other civil organizations has played a crucial role in bringing about a transformation, both in the government and in civil society.

The PSPD's activities in support of anti-corruption legislation started in January 1996 when it launched the Center for a Transparent Society campaign. For the past six years the PSPD has held public hearings, organized forums, lobbied through the National Assembly, conducted drives to collect signatures, -and campaigned jointly with the *Hankyoreh Daily* newspaper.

The anti-corruption bill drafted by the PSPD was a comprehensive countermeasure against corruption. It includes a public code of conduct, whistle-blower protection, measures against money laundering, appropriate punishments for corrupt behavior, and the establishment of the principle of independent counsel. For the 15th regular session of the National Assembly, which ended in 2000, the PSPD collected signatures from 256 of 299 National Assembly members who supported the PSPD's draft bill.

The establishment of a new administration in 1997 and the provision of aid from the International Monetary Fund boosted discourse about the need for an anti-corruption law. When they were out of office, the Millennium Democratic Party had submitted a bill similar to the PSPD's draft to the National Assembly. However, after the party came into power in 1997, it tried to omit the independent counsel concept and added exception regulations favorable to politicians. In 1999 the government set up the Special Commission on Anti-Corruption to prepare for the legislation. The commission consisted of representatives from various sectors, including nongovernment organizations (NGOs), and was thus in a position to gather diverse opinions about anti-corruption legislation; however, some of these opinions faced opposition from such government bodies as the Ministry of Justice and the Board of Audit and Inspection.

In June 2000, 38 civil organizations, including the PSPD, Transparency International Korea, and the Young Men's Christian Association, formed a coalition, Civil Action for the Enactment of the Anti-Corruption Law (Civil Action), to start full–scale lobbying activities.

In November 2000 the ruling party presented bills on anti-corruption and anti-money laundering to the National Assembly. The anti-corruption bill included provisions to protect and reward whistle-blowers and to establish a presidential commission on corruption prevention (now the Korea Independent Commission against Corruption). The commission would be concerned with whistle-blower protection, research, public education, and cooperation with NGOs. The opposition party, the Grand National Party, also submitted their bill, which included an independent counsel system, even though when the opposition had been in power it had opposed the independent counsel concept.

The central feature of the government's bill is its provision of systemic protection for those who report corrupt behavior. This is what civil organizations had wanted, that is, taking corruption control out of the exclusive hands of the government and encouraging the involvement of the public.

However, the bill has a number of problems. First, the proposed presidential commission on corruption prevention would not be powerful enough to oversee the policies of such central government bodies as the Ministry of Justice or the Board of Audit and Inspection.

Second, the bill does not include sufficient mechanisms for protecting whistleblowers. For example, if a whistle-blower faces retaliation, the bill specifies that it is up to the whistle-blower to prove that such retaliation took place instead of the whistle-blower's organization proving its action was not retaliatory. In addition, the bill does not consider retaliatory acts to be criminal offenses.

Third, the bill does not include provisions for an independent counsel system or a public code of conduct. One of the main features of the current system that enable corruption to continue is that the Prosecutor's Office is not impartial when investigating high-ranking officials, and fairness and impartiality have always been issues. This points to a need for reform of the Prosecutor's Office, especially the introduction of an independent counsel system. In addition, public officials need to be provided with a clear demarcation of what constitutes a gift and what is a bribe. Legal criteria and penalties to avoid having public officials find themselves in conflict of interest situations are urgently needed. The government maintains that existing principles already cover this problem, but civil organizations have doubts about the efficacy of these principles.

The anti-money laundering bill also has some problems. The first issue is whether or not the bill should introduce a currency transaction report system. Civil Action insisted on the need for such a report system in addition to the suspicious transaction report requirement; however, this demand was not reflected in the bill on the grounds that it might have a negative effect on the national economy.

The second issue was whether to allow the Financial Intelligence Unit to have access to financial transaction reports. Politicians opposed such access, because they were afraid of abuse of this regulation. A compromise in the final version of the bill permits access only after a warrant has been issued.

The third issue, a major problem, was an exception rule. The government's draft bill did not include regulations governing the laundering of illegal political funds. Faced by strong opposition to this exclusion by civil organizations Assembly members rectified this omission. However, a preferential rule was inserted in the draft that allows those whose financial transaction report is being investigation to receive prior notice. This obviously helps the suspect to destroy evidence or run away.

When the 16th regular session of the National Assembly opened in June 2000, Civil Action petitioned its version of the bill with the signatures of 208 out of 273 National Assembly members. Given the problems with the government's anti-corruption and anti-money laundering bills, Civil Action held public hearings. Civil Action also formed a monitoring group and provided comments on every deliberative council meeting.

Despite the issues raised by civil organizations, the anti-money laundering bill passed the National Assembly in April and the anti-corruption bill passed in June 2000 with only few changes. Thus careful monitoring of the enforcement of the law and a campaign to amend it are unavoidable.

The entire process of the passage of the Anti-Corruption Law provides a number of valuable lessons. To begin with, in the struggle against corruption the government needs to demonstrate a strong will to reform its bureaucratic systems, especially the Public Prosecutor's Office and the Board of Audit and Inspection. For civil society, closer and more careful National Assembly monitoring of the legislative process is also required to prevent politicians from changing proposed legislation in their favor. Finally, despite all the obstacles, cooperation between the proponents of reform in the government, politicians, and NGOs is crucial.

In the course of cooperation with the government NGOs can not only support the government during the course of policymaking, but at the same time they must play the role of critic and watchdog. During the course of cooperation with the government, NGOs must maintain their impartiality. When criticizing the government, NGOs need to take responsibility for the issues they have insisted on. The government for its part, needs to engage in dialogue with NGOs and listen to their point of view, whether or not the NGOs are cooperative, critical, or even hostile. Civil society will not be supportive of a government that is cooperative in appearance only.

Especially in most Asian countries, including Korea, NGOs need to be sound and responsible critics. It is important to monitor, check, and comment in these countries, because responsibility and transparency in politics and administration and impartiality and justice in judicial systems are urgently required. The question is "Who guards our guardians?" The answer is NGOs. When the government does not fulfill its role, strong criticism and persistent monitoring are indeed cooperation.

The fight against corruption is now indispensable. This fight is premised on cooperation between governments and civil society. In Korea, the inclusion of whistle-blower protection in the Anti-Corruption Law has extended anti-corruption activity to civil society as a whole. In addition, the passage of the Freedom of Information Act in 1998 has meant that citizens are increasingly monitoring the budgetary and policymaking processes of the central and local governments. In addition, actions are under way to permit intervention in the distorted corporate governance structure, for example, by means of class action lawsuits. Thus public action against corruption is on the rise, and in this sense passage of the Anti-Corruption Law was a sign of significant progress.

Nevertheless, pertinent legislation is not without its flaws. The Freedom of Information Act is cynically referred to as the Prevention of Access to Information Law, because those who seek information face a systematic lack of cooperation by public officials. The Integrity Pact also faces difficulties in relation to enforcement, because it does not include specific means for enforcing it. In the case of the Anti-Corruption Law, regulations on whistle-blowers are so strict that the law fails to provide actual protection. These drawbacks are due to the dual attitude of politicians, who adopt legislation to demonstrate their willingness to fight corruption, but try to ensure that it will not inhibit their own activities. NGOs in other countries may encounter similar problems.

This is why NGOs need to maximize their roles in society. They should be active in criticizing and in ensuring that opposition views are heard. In the course of policymaking -they should take the stance of an independent critic that does not hesitate to criticize a government for half-hearted policies. Then NGOs must evaluate and monitor the effects of systems that have already been put in place.

G. Society in Action Against Corruption

Chapter 15

The Asia Crime Prevention Foundation

■ **Minoru Shikita**

T he nongovernment organization (NGO) Asia Crime Prevention Foundation (ACPF) works to promote sustainable development, peace, and stability in Asia and the world through effective and humane crime prevention policies and practices and mutual cooperation among all those concerned. Its ultimate goal is to attain prosperity without crime. The ACPF currently has 28 branches throughout Japan and maintains ties with 50 affiliated organizations in Asia and other regions.

The ACPF was established in 1982 in Tokyo. Its creation was initiated by the United Nations Asia and Far East Institute for the Prevention of Crime and the Treatment of Offenders (UNAFEI), a United Nations (UN) regional training institute established in Tokyo in 1962. The ACPF's initial purposes were twofold: to help UNAFEI develop professional cadres and create a reservoir of knowledgeable leaders committed to positive change and to promote regional cooperation.

In 1991 the UN's Economic and Social Council awarded the ACPF special consultative status, and it became an official UN NGO. The ACPF is the first such organization in Asia specializing in crime prevention and criminal justice.

ACTIVITIES

The ACPF has made financial and technical contributions not only to the activities of UNAFEI and other affiliated organizations, but also to various UN projects, including UN experts meetings convened to draft UN norms and guidelines, for example, the UN Standard Minimum Rules for Noncustodial Measures (the Tokyo Rules). The ACPF has also contributed to various Economic and Social Commission for Asia and the Pacific crime-related projects, the most recent of which was the Model Project for Prevention of Juvenile Crime in the Community.

Since its inception, the ACPF has participated in all UN crime congresses, including regional and other preparatory meetings, as well as in other crime-related UN conferences, such as the 1994 World Ministerial Conference on Organized Transnational Crime. Indeed, the ACPF was the only NGO invited to attend the Asian Regional Ministerial Workshop on Organized Transnational Crime held in Manila in 1998.

In recognition of the importance of providing international forums for consultation and action, since 1992 the ACPF has organized the annual World Conference on Crime Prevention and Criminal Justice. Some 300 to 500 people from more than 20 countries generally attend the conferences, although 750 people from 69 countries attended the 2000 conference in Beijing. Conference themes have included such topics as conditions for prosperity without crime, effective regional cooperation in crime prevention and criminal justice, and crime prevention and criminal justice in the 21st century. The provision of such forums for consultation and action has proven to be particularly important in Asia, where unlike in other regions, no regular intergovernmental forums for criminal justice personnel are available.

One subject that has received particular attention during conference discussions is corruption. For example, during their discussion of the role of criminal justice in alleviating extreme poverty, participants at the eighth conference recognized corruption as the main cause of the deviation of funds intended for poverty alleviation. They identified ways and means for preventing the deviation of national financial resources and international aid or grants from the needy to the greedy as one of the key issues. The Beijing Declaration adopted at this conference reads in part as follows:

> Commit ourselves . . . to elaborating and implementing projects strengthening the capacity of law and criminal justice mechanisms to deal more imaginatively, resolutely, effectively and efficiently with criminal investigations of alleged corrupt officials acting above the law to the detriment of the poorest people and other victims of corruption.

At the same conference the subject of corruption was also discussed in the context of regional strategies for following up on the 10th UN Congress on the Prevention of Crime and the Treatment of Offenders and the role of prosecutors in a changing world. In this connection the Beijing Declaration states that the participants

Shall . . . promote best practices in combating corruption, including new legal arrangements, permitting the better detection, investigation and reporting of cases of bribery and corruption.

Shall encourage impartial investigation into cases of all alleged corruption, promote anti-corruption educational programmes and independent mass media coverage to help uncover corruption and enhance sentencing policies, developed in the context of the United Nations Code of Conduct for Public Officials and other international instruments.

The upcoming ACPF Working Group Meetings will examine these subjects further with the aim of elaborating comprehensive guidelines and initiating new activities to promote more active engagement by business and industry as well as the general public. In addition, because of the increasing globalization of crime, including corruption, there is a corresponding need for closer and more effective international cooperation in criminal matters. The ACPF has thus devoted its efforts to promoting and facilitating such cooperation by preparing the "Draft Model Convention for Asia and the Pacific Region on Mutual Assistance in Criminal Matters."

CHARACTERISTICS

The ACPF's activities reflect its characteristic features, namely:

- As its members are senior active or retired senior criminal justice personnel from each country, they reflect the informal but accurate wishes and intentions of their respective governments.
- Unlike many other NGOs, instead of merely protesting government actions the ACPF cooperates with governments and contributes to finding constructive and practical ways to improve the situation.
- ACPF members are familiar with different sectors of criminal justice and also represent other fields, such as civil society, business, and industry, thereby facilitating an integrated, systematic approach to problem solving.
- As an NGO, the ACPF can respond flexibly and swiftly to situations or problems that government agencies cannot always tackle.
- The use of a problem-solving approach helps raise public awareness regarding crime prevention and would be particularly effective in the fight against corruption.

STATUS UPGRADE

In May 2000 the UN Economic and Social Council reclassified the ACPF from special consultative status to general consultative status , one of only about 120 top category UN NGOs. As a result the ACPF is now qualified to propose agenda items for the Economic and Social Council and is to address wider socioeconomic issues, including sustainable development, the environment, the status of women, security, and so on, while maintaining its expertise in crime prevention and criminal justice.

Chapter 16

Increasing Information Access to Improve Political Accountability and Participation

■ **Gopakumar Krishnan**

> Knowledge will forever govern ignorance, and a people who mean to be their own governors must arm themselves with the power knowledge gives. A popular government without popular information or the means of acquiring it, is but a prologue to a farce or a tragedy or perhaps both.
>
> James Madison (as quoted in Meyers 1981)

Since the early 1990s, academic interest and activist movements on the theme of freedom of information have gained tremendous momentum. Today, one can showcase an interesting and inspiring range of models and initiatives that have used the key defining principles of this theme, either overtly in the form of legal provisions or subtly in the form of strategic campaigns.

This paper builds on a unique and concerted effort launched by the United Nations Development Programme (UNDP) in association with Transparency International, the OECD, and the ADB, with support from the United Kingdom's Department for International Development. The objective of this effort is to provide a forum for sharing good practices and ideas for improving political accountability and transparency through access to information. Key lessons learnt from this initiative were shared and discussed at a regional workshop organized under the auspices of the 10th International Anti-Corruption Conference held in Prague during 7-11 October 2001, and the discussion will be continued at this conference.

As a precursor to the Prague workshop, an online discussion was organized during August and September 2001 to prepare the groundwork for analyzing the concept of access to information and how such access improves accountability and transparency. This discussion paper heavily draws upon these discussions, but also includes information about well-documented and authenticated cases and good practices. (All quotes are from the online discussions unless otherwise indicated.)

CONCEPTUAL FOUNDATIONS AND DEFINITIONAL ISSUES

> While transparency and openness are in and of themselves desirable, the use of access to information is not neutral. It is an extremely powerful idea/issue/process/tool. The "who frames" and the "what" of the questions asked, determine the defining of its contours.
>
> Nikhil Dey, Mazdoor Kisan Shakthi Sanghatan

The strategic contours of access to information can be located within all contemporary discourses on good governance. At the core of these debates lie the principles of accountability, transparency, and participation, which are the basic tenets of democracy. As Dey observes:

> Rooting out inefficiency and corruption is viewed as the principal objective of openness and transparency in government. Access to information renders the processes of government more open and makes those in power more accountable to their people. Transparency in government ensures that citizens' interests are pursued and protected by those in power. Access to information is extremely important to the control of corruption but equally important for controlling the arbitrary exercise of power. This broader understanding allows access to information to be seen by citizens as a critical opening to their participation in democratic governance where they can not just ask questions but also have their opinions heard. Empowerment and participation will help ensure the involvement of ordinary people in decisions that affect their lives and enable them to build their strengths and assets.

Klitgaard (1988) has provided an interesting equation to explain corruption:

Corruption (C) = Monopoly (M) + Discretion (D) – Transparency (T).

Kiltgaard's simple arithmetic amplifies the distortionary and destructive potential of corruption as exemplified by the many cases of scams and scandals in the public sector. As history has repeatedly underscored, secrecy breeds corruption and the violation of human rights. Control of information in the hands of a powerful few has led to the marginalization of millions of people, who have been bypassed by development. Under such circumstances, access to information translates into a powerful tool for ensuring good governance and protecting human rights.

History is replete with instances of good concepts weakened by vague definitional parameters and the concomitant blurring of focus (see appendix I for a model freedom of information law). This is equally true in the case of the notion of access to information. So what exactly does access to information mean? Noted activist Dey responds:

> Access to information is the ability of citizens to obtain information about the past, present and future activities of the state. The phrase "freedom of information" is also widely used when referring to the ability of individuals to gain access to information in the possession of the state. Access to information is fundamentally about the quality of information available from the state, not the quantity. It has been argued that access to information is an essential element of democratic government. That is, for democracy to flourish, citizens must be adequately informed about the operations and policies of their government.

The basic premise of all ongoing debates on the issue of rights to information hinges around transactions between the state and its citizens, or how the abusive discretion of a monopoly state can be controlled and contested by the voices of an informed citizenry. However, Dey strongly argues for widening the ambit:

> The definition and scope of access to information should not be limited to the State. There are many non-state actors who are at least as powerful and their decisions have as much of an impact on people's lives as the State does. They also deal with public funds and their spheres of operations have a direct bearing on public interests. For instance, NGOs [nongovernment organizations], political parties, trade unions, companies and corporations, multi-nationals, service institutions like hospitals, international institutions, and international financial institutions. This has been a major bone of contention with the governments (State and Central) and their various drafts in the country, where all non-state actors have been left out of the purview of the acts. The argument given is that the State would be in a position to access the requisite information and provide it to the citizen. However, this argument we believe has been rightly contested because of the collusion that exists between the State and non-state actors, and

therefore we believe that both avenues should be open to citizens where they can access information directly from the organization concerned or through organs of the State.

Most legislation on access to information covers only state entities and omits critical nonstate entities like nongovernment organizations (NGOs), transnational corporations, funding agencies, and professional bodies. This is a glaring omission. As the world becomes increasingly enmeshed, global actors are playing an increasingly active role in local economies and societies. The current range of polemical themes, like bio-piracy (the poaching or exploitation of traditional flora, including medicinal herbs, for commercial gain), ethics and transparency in connection with the use of genetically modified foods, and dumping of hazardous waste, need to be covered under the rubric of access to information for any effective checks and balances to function.

Dey also points to the need for a wider debate on the different perspectives of access to information. He points out that the concept means different things to different people depending on their specific and broad objectives. Let us start by examining some of these differences and their implications.

EFFECTIVE STRATEGIES AND ENABLING IDEAS

While the world map profiling the implementation of effective access to information legislation presents a distressing scenario (figure 16.1), powerful ripples of innovative examples do exist (see annex II for a review of selected regional cases). Though most of these examples are context specific, the potential for effective cross-fertilization of ideas across borders is high. The components of an enabling environment include the following:

- *Political commitment and genuine intent.* A formally democratic political system may not be a sufficient condition for openness and transparency in government. Those in power must be willing to keep citizens informed of what is happening and must understand that citizens will exercise their rights to access information. When information is simply handed down "from above," it is likely to be more symbolic than real. While those in power often argue that open access to information leads to inefficiency and political instability, in practice the opposite is true.
- *Autonomy of the legal system.* If legislation governing access to information is to be enacted and successfully implemented, an independent judiciary must be in place. An independent judiciary is more likely to make decisions that may appear to go against the government's interests.

Figure 16.1

Access to Information Laws Around the World

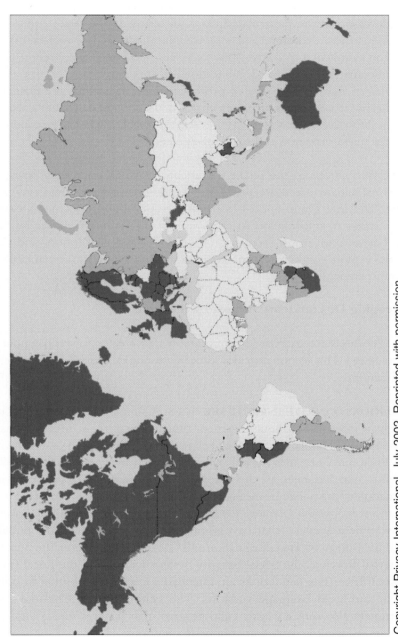

Copyright Privacy International, July 2002. Reprinted with permission.

Green – Access to Information Law Enacted
Yellow - Legislation Pending

- *Infrastructure.* Access to information involves both a personal and a state dimension. In relation to the individual, it involves aspects of personal development, in particular, literacy. In terms of the state, a physical infrastructure for travel and telecommunications needs to be established and maintained. Effective library services, accurate data collection, and information storage and publication are imperative.
- *Role of the media.* The state of professionalism, ownership, and financial health of a country's media are critical in the content of enabling access to information. Sensationalizing and irresponsible media can be conduits for misinformation and mass manipulation.

Contributions to the online discussions wove an interesting tapestry of regional initiatives and practices. This section breaks these down into two groups. The first group addresses petty corruption and documents cases linking access to information to challenges to discretionary abuses by the state. The second group focuses on so-called grand corruption, and the examples explore how access to information can lead to political accountability and transparency.

Challenging Discretionary Abuses by the State

The discretion exercised by a monopoly state creates powerful conduits for corruption. This section provides some interesting examples to help redress this situation.

HANDBOOKS ON GOVERNMENT SERVICES. A simple and effective way to disseminate information about the general functioning of the state is to publish handbooks about public services. The Fellowship of Christians in Government in the Philippines provides a good example of such an approach. Since 1999 the fellowship has been in the forefront of disseminating government information to the public by means of handbooks such as the *Basic Handbook of Government Standard Operating Procedures.* This particular handbook covers 12 government agencies that have significant interactions with the public, such as the Bureau of Trade Regulation and Consumer Protection, the Bureau of Internal Revenue, the Social Security System agency, and the Local Civil Registry Office. The handbooks are intended for wide distribution in both English and local language versions. The Fellowship of Christians in Government also runs a weekly radio program that features senior officials from various agencies answering phone-in questions.

STRENGTHENGING PUBLIC ACCOUNTABILITY THROUGH PUBLIC FEEDBACK. Observers often cite information barriers and asymmetry as major contributors to the widespread prevalence of systemic corruption. The situation is particularly acute in the relationship between monopoly services provided by the government and service recipients (citizens). Where alternative options do not exist, "voice mechanisms" become the only viable avenue for seeking improved responses and demanding greater accountability.

The report card system used by the Public Affairs Centre in Bangalore, India, and Transparency International Bangladesh confirm the value and effectiveness of public feedback mechanisms, both to enable citizens to signal service providers about their performance and to stimulate the latter to respond to these signals. A unique feature of the report card system is the way in which it focuses attention on corruption, which has always been difficult to pinpoint and quantify. Getting the givers of bribes to identify the agencies involved achieves a measure of specificity and credibility. Comparisons between agencies, locations, and so on attracts public attention and focuses public scrutiny on the agencies. The report card approach gives organized citizen groups the kind of information they need about corruption to seek reform in specific agencies and to demand greater public accountability

PARTICIPATORY BUDGETING PROCESSES. Increased citizen involvement in budgetary processes is an effective strategy for curbing corruption and increasing accountability. When an active citizenry starts questioning and scrutinizing budget provisions, accountability is bound to follow. Legislation is not required. All that is needed is committed collective action. For good case studies and examples see The International Budget Project's web site (http://www.internationalbudget.org/).

E-GOVERNANCE. A new and promising set of tools, combined under the rubric of e-governance, was highlighted by B. Shadrach from Loughborough University in the United Kingdom. These initiatives show much promise for an information-led anti-corruption strategy. Examples of regional initiatives that highlight the potential of this new avenue for improving accountability include the following:

- The national identification system in Egypt, which constitutes a comprehensive national database and aims to be an essential building block in public service planning and service delivery at the national level.
- The Info-Village project of the M. S. Swaminathan Foundation in India, which employs various technologies to create location-specific

knowledge systems. Recognizing the potential of this intervention, government authorities are willing to participate by providing government data.

- The Online Procedures Enhancement for Civil Applications system in metropolitan Seoul in the Republic of Korea informs the public and enables people to monitor the status of a variety of procedures, such as applications for permits and licenses.

The Gyandoot Program in Madhya Pradesh, India, is another example of effective decentralized governance using strategies enabled by information technology.

These examples of information and communication technology applications are easy to replicate and adaptable to any local context. However, to institutionalize and strengthen this process, an approach on three fronts is necessary, namely:

- Automating the laborious process of gathering, generating, and disseminating information for public consumption.
- Supporting the current process of using information for decisionmaking through e-governance applications by means of a collaborative approach between and within government departments and between NGOs, citizens, and the government.
- Creating technology processes enabled by information and communication technology that will engender changes in the public service delivery system. This may entail the development of legal frameworks to recognize e-signatures and e-applications.

Experiences from Japan reinforced the potential of information and communication technology for making government transactions more transparent. Many local governments in Japan use the Internet to generate public debate on budgetary provisions. In some cases the draft budget is put on web sites and the public is invited to send in comments. In other cases bidding and procurement procedures are put online.

PUBLIC HEARINGS. The concept of public hearings as a potent mechanism for demanding public accountability was highlighted through the experiences of *jan sunwais* (public hearings) pioneered by an Indian grassroots NGO, the Mazdoor Kisan Shakthi Sanghatan. *Jan sunwais* are essentially a public audit of development expenditures conducted by village residents. These hearings have the following four objectives:

- To assess the transparency of development expenditures
- To hold officials accountable
- To redress grievances
- To legitimize social or public audits.

This small experiment in a remote Indian village spearheaded a national campaign for the right to information across the country. For the first time the right to information emerged from the confines of intellectual debate and was defined by the poor as an issue related to their survival. The impact of public hearings has been dramatic. Local heads of public offices and bureaucrats were forced to attend, and when faced with proof of corruption, several offered public apologies and publicly returned stolen money. The demonstration effect has been encouraging: the fear of public exposure has reduced the levels of brazen corruption that were so prevalent in the recent past.

SUSTAINED INTERVENTIONS: FROM ACTIVISM TO LEGAL LITERACY. A clear disconnect is often apparent between the enactment of a law that guarantees access to information and the subsequent use of such a law. Quite often the legal provisions exist on paper, but its impacts on the ground are weak. A welcome departure from this disabling scenario is the work done by the Information Clearing House, Japan. This nonprofit, nongovernmental, and nonpartisan organization traces its origins to the Citizens' Movement for Information Disclosure, which was established in 1981 to campaign for the enactment of an information disclosure act. After 18 long years, such a law became reality in May 1999. The movement then got reorganized as the Information Clearing House, Japan, and has been educating the public on how to effectively use the provisions enshrined in the law through, for example, running an information center, carrying out surveys, bringing out publications, and organizing training programs. A novel concept initiated by the Clearing House, Japan was to set up a fund for information disclosure. The fund covers the fees for filing information disclosure requests and the costs of administrative and judicial appeals and of publishing materials.

Challenging the Opaqueness of Political Party Financing

Political party financing is widely perceived to be a major source of corruption. A good example is the Philippines where, according to Gico Dayanghirang, a member of the Coalition for Investment Promotion through Transparent Governance, political financing continues to come from the wealthy, special interest groups, and illegal sources. Thus areas of interest include responses to this situation, examples of legal provisions to control this form of corruption, the effectiveness of any such legal provisions, and the response of civil society constituents.

ENABLING LAWS. In Thailand, political parties are now required to disclose their financial accounts to the public, including donors' names. This new channel of information has facilitated a gradual increase in public awareness of the significance of transparency in politics. Khun Pokkrong Soontharasudth, deputy secretary general of Thailand's Election Commission, emphasizes the significance of this new legislation thus: "This new social character has made the politicians and persons who are holding positions in the state organization realize that they need to improve their performance to be more transparent and fairer. This is a good trend of political reform in Thailand." However, John Coronel of the Council of Asian Liberals and Democrats cautions as follows: "The peculiarities of Thai political culture appear to make any efforts to combat corruption, especially the corruption relating to electoral exercises, difficult, if not impossible, to gain ground."

RESEARCH AND DOCUMENTATION FOR CAPACITY BUILDING. The National Democratic Institute for International Affairs and the Council of Asian Liberals and Democrats have recently launched a regional program in Asia on Political Party Strategies to Combat Corruption. The program's purpose is to work with political parties to support their efforts to address "money politics" by promoting increased regional dialogue, sharing lessons learned, and identifying best practices.

In the first phase of this program, the National Democratic Institute for International Affairs and the Council of Asian Liberals and Democrats have been conducting comparative research on political parties' experiences with corruption. The research explores the challenges political parties face in dealing with money politics, gathers information about the specific strategies and tactics that parties have implemented to combat corruption, and will ultimately attempt to identify best practices that other parties facing similar challenges might use as a model. The bulk of the research comes from interviews with political party representatives from the major ruling and opposition parties in Cambodia; Indonesia; the Republic of Korea, Malaysia; Nepal; Philippines; Taipei,China; and Thailand. Information will also be gathered from similar interviews with civic leaders, government officials, election commissions, and independent bodies and from documents supplied by the parties, such as organizational charts, internal election procedures, manifestos, codes of conduct, and party education materials.

The main objective of the research is to try to identify concrete, detailed mechanisms that parties have implemented to reduce corruption within their ranks and to assess the effectiveness of these approaches. Such approaches may include codes of conduct, financial disclosure procedures, fundraising guidelines, ethical standards, internal party education and training programs, financial audit systems, and disciplinary procedures. To identify these mechanisms, the research is looking at such factors as the legal framework for political party financing and functioning, internal political party structures and decisionmaking practices, party fundraising strategies and accounting practices, party criteria for or standards of ethical conduct for members and enforcement mechanisms, and platform development and party discipline. From this research, the National Democratic Institute for International Affairs and the Council of Asian Liberals and Democrats will develop a manual for parties outlining anti-corruption strategies.

CIVIL SOCIETY RESPONSES. Given the scarcity of enabling legal provisions, one would have expected a strong response on the online discussion web site from various civil society constituents; however, this does not appear to be the case. To widen the range of possible options, some cases not covered by the online discussion are included in this section.

A good illustration of using legal provisions to monitor political processes effectively was highlighted by Pauline Tamesis of the UNDP. A Korean NGO, the People's Solidarity for Participatory Democracy, has used information garnered from members' of parliament declarations of assets and liabilities in their advocacy campaigns.

Lok Satta (People Power), an NGO based in Hyderabad, India, has a powerful forum, Election Watch, whose aim is to expose and curb electoral malpractice. Through an integrated approach starting with voter verification and registration, the forum uses a wide range of activist tools, such as screening candidates, organizing political debates, and monitoring polling. Under the leadership of Lok Satta, a network of civil society groups is actively advocating far-reaching electoral reforms, including voluntary disclosure of assets and state funding of elections.

The Public Affairs Centre, a nonprofit society based in Bangalore, India, has pioneered an interesting experiment on electoral transparency to help voters cast an informed vote. This initiative collects a range of information about candidates, such as the value of assets owned and criminal records, and then disseminates it to voters.

Bangladesh's Fair Elections Monitoring Alliance also carries out effective watchdog activities, whereby trained volunteers monitor the polling process and report on their findings.

FUTURE OPTIONS

Even though the need for legislation on access to information has been articulated strongly across the region, concrete action has been relatively weak. However, despite this situation, an interesting array of initiatives and ideas are present across the region and carry the seeds for change. The following paragraphs attempt to isolate some of these powerful strands to create a broad menu for action at the regional level. This discussion comes with a note of caution: these ideas were generated within a limited framework, and the hope is that this conference will further improve and broaden this agenda.

Regional Campaign for Access to Information

A regional campaign could be launched to promote the concept of access to information as a fundamental right. A good starting point for this initiative would be to identify model legislation that would incorporate all the critical themes that need to be addressed (see annex II). The campaign could be followed up with subregional workshops for a wide range of stakeholders, such as governments, civil society organizations, the media, elected representatives, corporate entities, and the donor community.

Research and Documentation

As many participants in the online discussions noted, there is a dearth of good research and documentation on the theme of access to information in the regional context. Some suggestions for redressing this situation include the following:

- *Developing a position paper for the region.* A comprehensive position paper could be prepared that discussed the current status of and impediments to legislating and operationalizing access to information provisions in various countries in the Asia–Pacific region. The paper could include existing good practices and success stories. As a precursor to this effort, country case studies could be developed to evaluate progress, as well as problems encountered in the implementation and operationalization of access to information laws.

- *Carrying out research on empirical links.* As Emiliano Bologatia succinctly illustrated in the online discussion, access to information by itself does not necessarily lead to corruption abatement. Much depends on how such access is linked to other institutional mechanisms, for example, democratic and pluralistic political processes and structures, media ownership, and political participation. In this context, another worthwhile endeavor would be to explore empirical links between access to information and indexes such as the Corruption Perception Index, the Economic Freedom Index, and the Human Rights Index. A good case in point in the regional context is the work done by Yvonne T. Chua of the Philippines Center for Investigative Journalism on eight Southeast Asian countries.
- *Creating a virtual regional resource center.* Such a center would be useful for pooling the diverse materials available and providing a forum for discussions and the sharing of experiences and ideas.

Capacity Building

In the context of capacity building, several approaches could be explored:

- *Workshops for parliamentarians.* Ensuring political will and commitment is essential for an effective policy on access to information. Focused workshops for parliamentarians and senior political representatives could be a potent intervention. The experiences of the Parliamentary Centre, Ottawa, bear ample testimony to utility of such an approach. The experiences could also be shared through a regional platform.
- *Workshops for media representatives.* As a critical link in the process, the media need to be sensitized to emergent concerns and applicable tools. The World Bank's series of media workshops on fighting corruption provide a good model.
- *Workshops for civil society groups.* Public interest groups and civil society organizations need to be made aware of the powerful techniques available for mobilizing demand and of such tools as public hearings and social audits.

To sustain such capacity building initiatives, information kits and advocacy materials need to be prepared and made available to interested groups.

Networking and Coalitions

Coalitions can provide powerful leverage for advocacy. A broadly based, multistakeholder coalition can be a powerful platform for regional policy dialogues and advocacy. Such coalitions can be built onto existing forums, like the UNDP's PARAGON regional governance program and the ADB/OECD Anti-Corruption Initiative for Asia-Pacific. In addition to knowledge networking and dialogues, coalitions can also actively launch regional campaigns on pertinent themes such as electoral reform.

Impact Evaluation

Regional surveys can be undertaken to evaluate the progress of various initiatives and programs, and also to benchmark comparative statistics across the region. The surveys can focus on such issues as the level of awareness about access to information provisions among various stakeholders, the practical relevance of such provisions, and the actual use made of the provisions. A new approach that can be tried out is to create an index of political will that would measure the commitment of governments in the region to enact and implement access to information laws. A good reference point for this is the work Social Watch has done to monitor the commitments made by different governments at various United Nations conferences.

ANNEX I
FRAMEWORK FOR A MODEL FREEDOM OF INFORMATION LAW

The following is an outline of the possible arrangement of sections within the various parts of a model freedom of information law.

Part I: Definitions and Purpose

    1. Definitions
    2. Purpose

Part II: The Right to Access Information Held by Public Bodies

    3. Freedom of Information
    4. General Right of Access
    5. Legislation Prohibiting or Restricting Disclosure
    6. Public and Private Bodies
    7. Records
    8. Request for Information
    9. Time Limits for Responding to Requests
    10. Notice of Response
    11. Fees
    12. Means of Communicating Information
    13. If a Record Is Not Held
    14. Vexatious, Repetitive, or Unreasonable Requests

Part III: Measures to Promote Openness

    15. Guide to Using the Act
    16. Information Officer
    17. Duty to Publish
    18. Guidance on Duty to Publish
    19. Maintenance of Records
    20. Training of Officials
    21. Reports to the Information Commissioner

Part IV: Exceptions

    22. Public Interest Override
    23. Information Already Publicly Available

Part IX: Miscellaneous Provisions

50. Regulations

51. Interpretation
52. Short Title and Commencement

Source: Adapted from Centre for Policy Alternatives (2001).

APPENDIX II
ACCESS TO INFORMATION IN SELECTED ASIA-PACIFIC COUNTRIES

A glance at the status of access to information provisions in Asia and the Pacific reveals some interesting variations.

Australia

The 1982 federal Freedom of Information Act provides for access to government records. The Commonwealth ombudsman promotes the act and handles complaints about procedural failures. Merits review (appeals) of adverse freedom of information decisions are provided by the Administrative Appeals Tribunal, with the possibility of further appeals on points of law to the federal court. However, budget cuts have severely restricted the capacity of the Attorney General's Department and the ombudsman to support the act, and little central direction, guidance, or monitoring are now available. The government has announced an extension of the act to cover contracted service providers, but a bill has not yet been introduced. All the states and the ACT, but not the Northern Territory, also have freedom of information laws that include rights for individuals to gain access to and to correct personal information about themselves.

Hong Kong, China

The Code on Access to Information requires civil servants to provide records held by government departments unless they have specific reasons for not doing so. Departments can withhold information if it relates to 16 different categories, including defense, external affairs, law enforcement, and personal privacy. Formal complaints about denials can be filed with the ombudsman. The code is not considered to be very effective.

India

In 1982 the Supreme Court ruled that access to government information was an essential part of the fundamental right to freedom of speech and expression. A draft freedom of information act was presented to Parliament in July 2000. The bill would provide for a general right to access information and create the National Council for Freedom of Information and state councils. The bill contains seven broad categories of exemptions. The draft was heavily criticized by campaigners, who said that the bill provided only limited access to government records. The National Centre for Advocacy Studies said: "Many of the aspects towards information availability have been left completely in the hands of bureaucrats, which defeats the very purpose of the bill." NGO representatives estimated that the bill would be approved in mid-2001. In 1997 the state of Tamil Nadu adopted the Act for Right to Information and the states of Gujarat and Rajasthan have administratively provided access to records. The state of Madhya Pradesh enacted the Right to Information Bill in March 1998.

Indonesia

The Coalition for Information Freedom, a group of 17 NGOs, released a draft freedom of information act in February 2001 and planned to present it to Parliament the following month. The draft act sets broad rights for access by any person to information held by government agencies, legislative and judicial bodies, state-owned companies, NGOs receiving public funding, and private companies conducting government activities. Government bodies are obligated to maintain and disseminate information, but can withhold it for reasons pertaining to law enforcement, intellectual property, national defense and security, health and safety, or confidentiality about individuals. The act creates a central information commission and regional information commissions to oversee the act. The commission can overrule the withholding of information if disclosing the information is in the public interest.

Japan

The Diet approved the Disclosure of Information Act in May 1999 after 20 years of debate, and the law went into effect in 2001. The law allows any individual or company to request government information in electronic or printed form. A nine-person committee in the Office of the Prime Minster receives complaints about information that the government refuses to make public and examines whether such decisions were appropriate. Government officials still have broad discretion to refuse requests, but requesters can appeal such decisions to withhold documents to one of eight different district courts. A survey by the *Kyodo News* in May 1999 found that 31 city and prefectural governments were in the process of adopting legislation consistent with the new law.

Republic of Korea

In 1989 the Supreme Court ruled that the public has a constitutional right to information "as an aspect of the right of freedom of expression, and specific implementing legislation to define the contours of the right was not a prerequisite to its enforcement." The Act on Disclosure of Information by Public Agencies is a freedom of information act that allows Koreans to demand access to government records. It was enacted in 1996 and went into effect in 1998.

Nepal

In June 2000, a delegation of journalists presented Information and Communication Minister Jaya Prakash Prasad Gupta with a draft freedom of information bill, and asked him to present it to Parliament. The bill provides for a broad right of access to official information and information on the performance of political parties, NGOs, and companies. The bill also requires officials to periodically disclose information and keep systematic records. Officials who refuse to comply with requests can be fined US$75.

New Zealand

The 1982 Official Information Act and the 1987 Local Government Official Information and Meetings Act are freedom of information legislation governing the public sector. The Office of the Ombudsman supervises enforcement. The links between this freedom of information legislation and the Privacy Act in relation to subject matter, administration, and jurisprudence are so extensive that the three sets of provisions can be viewed as complementary components of a single statutory scheme.

Pakistan

In August 2000 the federal minister for information released a draft freedom of information ordinance. The draft, which is based on a 1997 ordinance that was never adopted, provides for broad exemptions, including the notes officials place on files, minutes of meetings, interim orders, classified records (with no limits on classification), and records relating to the personal privacy of any individual. Government officials have broad discretion to determine if the requester is "fit" to obtain the information, and no penalties are incurred for refusing to comply. The draft has been heavily criticized by commentators. Arif Nizami, president of the Council of Pakistan Newspaper

Editors, said that the revisions make the already weak 1997 ordinance even weaker. The International Press Institute wrote that "the Ordinance is a lacklustre attempt at providing a freedom of information law in Pakistan and displays little commitment on the part of the ruling authorities to practice open and honest government" (cited in Banisar 2001).

Philippines

The 1987 Constitution states: "The right of the people to information of matters of public concern shall be recognized. Access to official records and documents, and papers pertaining to official acts, transactions, or decisions as well as to government research data used as a basis for policy development, shall be afforded the citizen, subject to such limitations as may be provided by law." The Code of Conduct and Ethical Standards for Public Officials and Employees mandates the disclosure of public transactions and guarantees access to official information, records, or documents. Agencies must act on a request within 15 working days from receipt of the request. Complaints against public officials and employees who fail to act on a request can be filed with the Civil Service Commission or the Office of the Ombudsman.

Thailand

The Thai Constitution states: "Persons shall have the right to receive information or news from the government agency or state agency or public enterprise in order to check the performance of the government official or state official when such matters have or may have affects on the living of such person as the law provided." The Official Information Act was approved in July 1997 and went into effect in December 1997. The act allows citizens to obtain government information such as the result of a decision that has a direct effect on a private individual, a work plan, a project and the project's annual expenditure estimates, and manuals or orders relating to work procedures of state officials that affect the rights and duties of private individuals. The Official Information Commission oversees the act. Individuals can appeal denials to the commission. According to the commission, 113 complaints were registered in 1999, of which 80 were resolved and the remaining 33 are being processed. The commission noted a number of problems with implementing the new act, including the following:

- Most people do not understand key elements of the act or their own rights. Most people do not know how to use the law to meet their demands for access to state information. Thus people cannot exercise their rights, because they do not know the procedures to use.

- Senior officials in government agencies do not understand the law and do not know how to implement the act. They lack adequate knowledge of the law and are unfamiliar with the main principles of information disclosure, and are thus unable to comply with the act.
- Lower-level staff in government agencies are also insufficiently informed about the act and are not used to the new principles of information disclosure. They also have negative attitudes toward the act, in that some feel that it simply adds to their burden.

In October 2000, the Supreme Court upheld an order by the Official Information Commission to disclose school entrance examination results demanded by parents of children who were rejected by an elite elementary school. According to media reports, in November 2000 the Cabinet approved a measure that prohibits confidentiality clauses in government contracts.

Source: Adapted from Banisar (2001).

REFERENCES

Banisar, David. 2001. *Freedom of Information and Access to Government Records around the World*. Privacy International. (On-line). Available: http:// www.privacyinternational.org/issues/foia/FOI_survey3.01.pdf.

Centre for Policy Alternatives. 2001. *A Model Freedom of Information Law*. Commonwealth Human Rights Initiative and Human Rights Commission of Pakistan. (On-line). Available: http://www.article19.org.

Klitgaard, Robert. 1988. *Controlling Corruption*. Berkeley and Los Angeles, California: University of California Press.

Meyers, Mervin. 1981. *The Mind of the Founder: Sources of the Political Thought of James Madison*. Hanover, New Hampshire.

APPENDICES

PARTICIPANTS

CONTRIBUTORS

Mr. Rainer Geiger

Deputy Director
Directorate for Financial, Fiscal and Enterprise Affairs
Organisation for Economic Co-operation and Development
2, rue André Pascal
F-75775 Paris Cedex 16
France
Tel: +33 1 45 24 91 03
Email: rainer.geiger@oecd.org

Mr. Omkar Goswami

Chief Economist
Confederation of Indian Industry
23 Institutional Area, Lodi Road
New Delhi 110003
India
Tel: +91 11 4601081
Fax: +91 11 4626449
Email: omkar.goswani@ciionline.org

Mr. Toshio Kojima

Parliamentary Secretary
Ministry of Foreign Affairs
Shiba Koen 2-11-1, Minato-Ku, Tokyo 105-8519
Japan
Tel: +81 3 3580 3311
Fax: +81 3 3581 9470

Mr. Seiichi Kondo

Deputy Secretary-General
Organisation for Economic Co-operation and Development
2, rue André Pascal
F-75775 Paris Cedex 16
France
Tel: +33 1 45 24 80 30
Email: seiichi.kondo@oecd.org

Dr. Gopakumar Krishnan
Programme Manager for Asia
International Secretariat
Transparency International
Berlin
Tel: +49 30 343 8200
Fax: +49 30 347 03912
Email: gkrishnan@transparency.org; gopa66@yahoo.com

Mr. Taeho Lee
Director, Transparency & Accountability Department
PSPD, People's Solidarity for Participatory Society
3F Anguk New B/D., 175-3 Anguk-Dong Chongno-Gu
Seoul 110-240
Republic of Korea
Tel: +82 2 723 5302
Fax: +82 2 723 5055
Email: gaemy@pspd.org

Mr. Guan Eng Lim
National Vice-Chair
Democratic Action Party Malaysia
106 MT Ujong Pasir, Sinn Garden
75050 Malacca
Malaysia
Tel: +60 6 2829780
Fax: +60 6 2829816
Email: limge@tm.net.my

Mr. Sum Manit
Secretary of State
Secretary-General of the Council of Administrative Reform
P.O. Box 1270, Phnom Penh
Cambodia
Tel: +855 12 806 622
Fax: +855 23 880 627
Email: tinamus@camnet.com.kh

The Hon. Mr. Justice Barry O'Keefe AM
Supreme Court of New South Wales
Law Courts Building, Queens Square
184 Phillip St., Sydney 2000
Australia
Tel: +61 2 9228 8167
Fax: +61 2 9228 7164
Email: justice_okeefe@courts.nsw.gov.au

Ms. Devendra Raj Panday
President
Transparency International Nepal
P.O. Box 11486, Kathmandu
Nepal
Tel: +977 1 436 462
Fax: +977 1 420 412
Email: trans@tinepal.org

Mrs. Enery Quinones
Head
Anti-Corruption Division
Directorate for Financial, Fiscal and Enterprise Affairs
Organisation for Economic Co-operation and Development
2, rue André Pascal
F-75775 Paris Cedex 16
France
Tel: +33 1 45 24 91 02
Fax: +33 1 44 30 63 07
Email: enery.quinones@oecd.org

Mr. Minoru Shikita
Chairman, Board of Directors
Asia Crime Prevention Foundation
602 Bureau, 1-7-16-Hirakawa-cho
Chiyoda-ku, Tokyo 102-0093
Japan
Tel: +81 3 3238 1399
Fax: +81 3 3238 1370
Email: shikita@acpf.org

Prof. Narayanan Srinivasan
Dean
Murdoch Business School
Murdoch University
South Street, Murdoch
Western Australia
Tel: +61 8 9400 5407
Fax: +61 8 9400 5633
Email: n.srinivasan@ecu.edu.au

Mr. Gerald A. Sumida
General Counsel
Office of the General Counsel
Asian Development Bank
6 ADB Avenue, Mandaluyong City, 0401 MM
P.O. Box 789, 0980 Manila, Philippines
Tel: +632 632 4890
Fax: +632 636 2501
Email: gsumida@adb.org

Mr. Yuichiro Tachi
Professor
United Nations Training Cooperation Department,
Research and Training Institute, Ministry of Justice
1-26, Fuchuu-si, Harumi-cho,
Tokyo 183-0057
Japan
Tel: +81 42 333 4604
Fax: +81 42 333 4656
Email: yt000296@moj.go.jp

Mr. Tolondu Toichubaev
Chairman
Corporate Technologies Centre
28A, 8 District, 8F
Southgate Business Center, 720075 Bishkek
Kyrgyz Republic
Tel: +996 312 512300
Fax: +996 312 512302
Email: ttoichubaev@ctc.kg

Mr. Clay Wescott
Senior Public Administration Specialist
Asian Development Bank
6 ADB Avenue, Mandaluyong City, 0401 MM
P.O. Box 789, 0980 Manila, Philippines
Tel: +632 632 5680
Fax: +632 636 2193
Email: cwescott@adb.org

Mr. Akira Yamada
Counselor
Secretariat of Information Disclosure Review Board
Tel: +81 3 5501 1717
Fax: +81 3 3502 0035
Email: ayamada@op.cao.go.jp

Mr. Shomei Yokouchi
Vice-Minister of Justice
Ministry of Justice
1-1-1 Kasumigaseki Chiyoda-ku Tokyo 100-8977
Japan
Tel: +81 3 3580 4111
    ext. 2373, 2374
Fax: +81 3 3592 7034

Ms. Zohra Yusuf
Council Member
Human Rights Commission of Pakistan
Flat 4, 19/F Block 6
PECHS, Karachi
Pakistan
Tel: +9221 4546117
Fax: +9221 5882328/ 5882197
Email: zyusuf@cyber.net.pk

DELEGATES

ARGENTINA

Mr. Fernando Higa
Counselor
Embassy of the Argentine Republic
2-14-14, Moto-Azabu, Minato-ku
Tokyo 106-0046, Japan
Tel: +81 3 5420 7101
Fax: +81 3 5420 7109
Email: ejapo@mb.rosenet.nejp

AUSTRALIA

Mr. Gregory Andrews
Director, Development Policy
AUSAID
Australian Embassy
2-4-14 Mita Minato ku
Tokyo 108-8361, Japan
Tel: +81 3 3581 3871
Fax: +81 3 5232 4140
Email: zamininduu@yahoo.com

Mr. Peter Rooke
Member of the Board
Transparency International –Australia
PO Box A2327
Sydney South
NSW 1235
Tel: +612 9326 1737
Fax: +612 9327 8480
Email: prooke@transparency.org.au

BANGLADESH

Mr. Manzoor Hasan
Executive Director
Transparency International Bangladesh
3/F, 121C Gulshan Avenue
Dhaka-1212
Tel: +880 2 882 6036
Fax: +880 2 988 4811
Email: ed@ti-bangladesh.org

Dr. Abdul Moyeen Khan
Minister for Science and Information & Communication Technology
Ministry of Science and Information & Communication Technology
Rm. 812, Building 4, Bangladesh Secretariat
Dhaka
Tel: +880 2 861 6229/6230
Fax: +880 2 861 6231
Email: amk_mp@proshikanet.com

Mr. Enayetullah Khan
Publisher and Editor-in-Chief
Holiday
The Holiday Building
30 Tejgaon Industrial Area
Dhaka-1208
Tel: +880 2 912 2950/8117
Fax: +880 2 912 7927
Email: holiday@bangla.net

BELGIUM

Ambassador Gustaaf Dierckx
Embassy of the Kingdom of Belgium
Chancery: 5, Niban-cho
Chiyoda-ku, Tokyo 102-0084, Japan
Tel: +81 3 3262 0191/5
Fax: +81 3 3262 0651

CHILE

Mr. Rodrigo Arcos
Embassy of the Republic of Chile
8/F Nihon Seimei Akabanebashi Building
3-1-14, Shiba, Minato-ku, Tokyo 105-0014
Japan
Tel: +81 3 3452 7561/7585
Fax: +81 3 3452 4457
Email: rarcos@chile.or.jp

COOK ISLANDS

Mr. Kevin Carr
Financial Secretary
Ministry of Finance and Economic Management
PO Box 41, Rarotonga
Tel: +682 22 878/879
Fax: +682 23 877/21 511
Email: finsec@oyster.net.ck

EUROPEAN COMMISSION

Mr. Horst M. Pilger
Programme Manager, Institutional Support for Asia
EuropeAid Coop. Office
200, Rue de la Loi
B-1049 Brussels
Tel: +32 2 299 2717
Fax: +32 2 296 4831
Email: Horst.Pilger@cec.eu.int

FIIJ ISLANDS

Mr. Ralulu Cirikiyasawa
Principal Auditor
Policy Compliance and Audit
Ministry of Finance
P.O. Box 2122, Government Buildings, Suva
Tel: +679 307 011
Fax: +679 308 654
Email: rcirikiyasawa@govnet.gov.fj

Mr. Daryl Tarte
Executive Committee Member
Transparency International
PO Box 12007, Suva
Tel: +679 322 405
Fax: +679 322 405
Email: tartedv@is.com.fj

FRANCE

Mr. Jean-Yves Parssegny
Financial Attaché
French Embassy in Tokyo
1-23-5, Higashi Azabu
Minato-ku, Tokyo 106-0044, Japan
Tel: +81 3 3582 7432
Fax: +81 3 3582 0490
Email: message@afitokyo.or.jp

HONG KONG, CHINA

Mr. Paul Mackellar
Leader
KPMG Forensic Greater China
27/F, Alexandra House
16-20 Chater Road
Central, Hong Kong
Tel: +852 3121 9868
Fax: +852 3121 9868
Email: Paul.Mackellar@kpmg.com.hk

INDIA

Mr. Bhaskar Khulbe
Director
Department of Personnel and Training
Ministry of Personnel, Public Grievances and Pensions
Room 19A, North Block, New Delhi 110-001
Tel: +91 11 304 1842
Fax: +91 11 301 3063
Email: bkhulbe123@hotmail.com

Mr. Sunil Krishna
Executive Director (Vigilance)
Krishak Bharati Cooperative Limited
A-8-10, Sector 1
Noida-201301
Tel: +91 118 453 4635
Fax: +91 118 454 9342
Email: sunil_krishna@vsnl.com

Admiral R.H. Tahiliani
Chairman
Transparency International - India
Lajpat Bhawan, Lajpat Nagar
New Delhi – 110024
Tel: +91 11 622 4711
Fax: +91 11 463 8899
Email: tindia@ndf.vsnl.net.in or tiindia@hotmail.com

INDONESIA

Mr. Romli Atmasasmita
Director General
Legal Administrative Affairs
Jl. H.R. Rasuna Said Kav. 6-7 Kuningan
Jakarta
Tel: +62 21 520 2391
Fax: +62 21 526 1082
Email: kumdang@indosat.net.id

Mr. Mukti Asikin
Secretary-General
PUPUK (The Association for The Advancement of Small Business)
Jalan Permata Bumi Raya, Kav.6
Arcamanik Bandung 40293
Tel: +62 22 783 4483
Fax: +62 22 788 4484
Email: mukti@adbtasme.or.id

Dr. Emil P. Bolongaita, Jr.
Assistant Professor
The Public Policy Programme
Faculty of Arts and Social Sciences
National University of Singapore
AS7 Shaw Foundation Building Level 6
Singapore 117570
Tel: +65 874 6794
Fax: +65 778 1020
Email: mppeb@nus.edu.sg

Mr. Agus Haryanto
Inspector General
Ministry of Finance
Jl. Dr. Wahidin No. 1, Jakarta
Tel: +62 21 319 01 53
Fax: +62 21 314 3731

Ms. Irma Hutabarat
Chair
Institute for Civic Education on Indonesia (ICE)
Jl. Kemang Barat No. 10 H
Jakarta Selatan 12730
Tel: +62 21 717 91 743
Fax: +62 21 717 91 154
E-mail: irma@basmikorupsi.org

Mr. Teten Masduki
Chief of Working Committee
Indonesia Corruption Watch
Jalan Tulodong Bawah 9
Kebayoran Baru, Jakarta Seletan
Tel: +62 21 919 5974/ 526 5066
Fax: +62 21 573 6448
Email: icwmail@rad.ned.id

Mr. Eddy Purwanto
Assistant to Deputy Minister for International Economic Cooperation
The Coordinating Ministry for Economic Affairs
Jalan Taman Suropati 2, Jakarta
Tel: +62 21 319 01 153
Fax: +62 21 314 37 31

JAPAN

Mr. Katsuhide Ariyoshi
Senior Assistant
Ministry of Foreign Affairs
2-2-1 Kasumigaseki, Chiyoda-ku, Tokyo 100-8919
Tel: +81 3 3580 3311 ext. 3215
Fax: +81 3 3580 9319
Email: katsuhide.ariyoshi@mofa.go.jp

Mr. Julius Court
Programme Officer
Office of the Rector
United Nations University
5-53-70 Jingumae, Shibuya-ku
Tokyo, T 150-8925
Tel: +81 3 5467 1220
Fax: +81 3 3499 2810
Email: court@hq.unu.edu

Mr. Garron Elders
Managing Director
Hill & Associates Japan K.K.
New Horizon Ebisu Building
3-14-20 Higash, Shibuya-ku, Tokyo 150-0011
Tel: +81 3 5766 6848
Fax: +81 3 5766 5849
Email: garron.elders@hill-assoc.com

Ms. Chikako Fujii
Special researcher
House of Councillors First Research Office
1-11-16 Nagatacho, Chiyoda-ku, Tokyo 100-0014
Tel: +81 3 3581 3111 ext. 3154
Fax: +81 3 5512 3915
Email: chikako.fujii@sangiin.go.jp

Mr. Hiroshi Fujiwara

Special Coordinator
Japan External Trade Organization(JETRO)
2-2-5 Toranomon, Minato-ku, Tokyo 105-8466
Tel: +81 3 3582 5196
Fax: +81 3 3583 0754
Email: Fujiwara_Hiroshi@jetro.go.jp

Mr. Kenji Fukuda

Advocacy Coordinator
Mekong Watch Japan
5/F Marukou Building
1-20-6 Higashiueno, Taitou–ku, Tokyo 110-8605
Tel: +81 3 3832 5034
Fax: +81 3 5818 0520
Email: fukudan@sol.dti.ne.jp

Mr. Hideki Goda

Chief Remuneration Research Officer
National Personnel Authority
1-1-1Kasumigaseki, Chiyoda-ku, Tokyo 100-8913
Tel: +81 3 3581 5311
Fax: +81 3 3580 2960
Email: GODA-H@jinji.go.jp

Mr. Yasunori Goke

Intellectual Property Policy Office Unit-Chief
Ministry of Economy,Trade and Industry
1-3-1 Kasumigaseki, Chiyoda-ku, Tokyo 100-8901
Tel: +81 3 3501 3752
Fax: +81 3 3501 6046
Email: goke-yasunori@meti.go.jp

Mr. Yoichiro Hamabe

Lawyer
Hamada Matsumoto Law Firm
25/F Kasumigaseki Building
2-5, Kasumigaseki 3-chome, Chiyoda-ku, Tokyo 100-6025
Tel: +81 3 3580 3377
Fax: +81 3 3581 4713
Email: Hamabe@h-m.chiyoda.tokyo.jp

Mr. Akio Hayashi
President
Kairin Juku School
145 Horikomicyou Ashikaga-shi, Tochigi 326-0831
Tel: +81 284 72 5945
Fax: +81 284 73 1520
Email: akio@kairin.co.jp

Mr. Masayuki Hanai
General Manager
Legal Department
Nissho Iwai Corporation
2-3-1 Daiba, Minato-ku, Tokyo 135-8655
Tel: +81 3 5520 2748
Fax: +81 3 5520 2724
Email: hanai.masayuki@nisshoiwai.co.jp

Mr. Keiji Ide
Director
Regional Policy Division
Asian and Oceanian Affairs Bureau
Ministry of Foreign Affairs
Shiba Koen 2-11-1, Minato-Ku, Tokyo 105-8519
Tel: +81 3 3580 3311
Fax: +81 3 3581 9470

Mr. Ichiro Ishii
Deputy Manager
Maeda Corporation
2-10-26 Fujimi, Chiyoda-ku, Tokyo 102-8151
Tel: +81 3 5276 5154
Fax: +81 3 3262 3339
Email: ishiii@jcity.maeda.co.jp

Mr. Hiromichi Jitsuno
Manager
Legal Department
Sumitomo Corporation
1-8-11 Harumi, Chuou-ku, Tokyo 104-0053
Tel: +81 3 5166 3583
Fax: +81 3 5166 6207
Email: hiromichi.jitsuno@sumitomocorp.co.jp

Mr. Shinji Kadooka
Inspector
Second International Affairs Div, International Affairs Department
National Police Agency of Japan
2-1-2 Kasumigaseki Chiyoda-ku Tokyo 100-8974
Tel: +81 3 3581 0141
Fax: +81 3 3580 5091
Email: mtanaka01@npa.go.jp

Ms. Maki Kataoka
Inspector
Second Investigation Div, Criminal Investigation Bureau,
National Police Agency of Japan
2-1-2 Kasumigaseki, Chiyoda-ku, Tokyo 100-8974
Tel: +81 3 3581 0141
Fax: +81 3 3580 5091
Email: mtanaka01@npa.go.jp

Mr. Gaku Kato
Research Fellow
Institute of Developing Economies, IDE-JETRO
3-2-2 Wakaba, Mihama-ku, Chiba-shi Chiba 261-8545
Tel: +81 43 299 9608
Fax: +81 43 299 9729
Email: g-kato@ide.go.jp

Mr. Yasuhisa Kawamura
Director
Ministry of Foreign Affairs
2-2-1Kasumigaseki, Chiyoda-ku, Tokyo 100-8919
Tel: +81 3 3580 3311
Fax: +81 3 3581 9470
Email: yasuhisa.kawamura@mofa.go.jp

Ms. Yukiko Kawasugi
Liaison Officer
Minister's Secretariat Division
Ministry of Justice
1-1-1   Kasumigaseki, Chiyoda-ku, Tokyo 100-8977
Tel: +81 3 3592 7004
Fax: +81 3 3592 7011
Email: yk990137@moj.go.jp

Mr. Keiichi Kimura
Assistant Director
Special Coordinator Office
Japan External Trade Organization(JETRO)
2-2-5 Toranomon, Minato-ku, Tokyo 105-8466
Tel: +81 3 3582 5196
Fax: +81 3 3583 0754
Email: Keiichi_Kimura@jetro.go.jp

Ms. Mikie Kiyoi
Director
International Research Cooperation
National Institute for Research Advancement
34/F Ebisu Garden Place
4-20-3 Ebisu, Shibuya-ku, Tokyo 150-6034
Tel: +81 3 5448 1714
Fax: +81 3 5448 1744
Email: mkiyoi@nira.go.jp

Mr. Kikufumi Konishi
2-16-9 Nakahara Mitaka
Tokyo 181-0005
Tel: +81 422 49 3808
Fax: +81 422 49 3808
Email: cpi_mate@muh.biglobe.ne.jp

Mr. Sadaaki Koyama
Private Secretary to the Senior Vice-Minister of Justice
Ministry of Justice
1-1-1 Kasumigaseki, Chiyoda-ku, Tokyo 100-8977
Tel: +81 3 3580 4111
    ext. 2373, 2374
Fax: +81 3 3592 7034

Ms. Kiyo Kudo
Assistant Director
National Police Agency (International Affairs Department)
2-1-2 Kasumigaseki, Chiyoda-ku, Tokyo 100-8974
Tel: +81 3 3581 0141 ext. 2976
Fax: +81 3 3580 3557

Mr. Tatsuro Kuroda
Director General
The Freedom of Information Citizen's Center
2/F Hashizume Building
Miecyou Shinjyuku-ku, Tokyo 160-0008
Tel: +81 3 5368 1520
Fax: +81 3 5368 1521
Email: kurodatk@dd.mbn.or.jp

Mr. Ikuo Kuroiwa
Senior Research Fellow
Economic Cooperation Research Department
Institute of Developing Economies
Japan External Trade Organization
3-2-2 Wakaba, Mihama-ku, Chiba-shi Chiba 261-8545
Tel: +81 43 299 9613
Fax: +81 43 299 9731
Email: kuroiwa@ide.go.jp

Mr. Timothy Langley
General Counsel and Director of Public Policy
General Motors Asia-Pacific Japan
Yebisu Garden Place Tower
27/F 4-20-3 Ebisu, Shibuya-ku, Tokyo 150-6027
Tel: +81 3 5424 2985
Fax: +81 3 5424 2848
Email: tlangley@gmjapan.co.jp

Mr. Kazutoshi Maeda
Deputy General Manager
Legal Division
Itochu Corporation
2-5-1 Kitaaoyama, Minato-ku, Tokyo 107-8077
Tel: +81 3 3497 4032
Fax: +81 3 3497 4039
Email: maeda-ka@itochu.co.jp

Ms. Yukiko Miki
Executive Director
Information Clearinghouse Japan
Kiunnkaku Building 108

3 Aizumicho Shinjyuku-ku, Tokyo 106-0005
Tel: +81 3 5269 1846
Fax: +81 3 5269 0944
Email: yukiko.miki@nifty.com

Mr. Takeshi Mine

Head of International Affairs
Japan Chemical Industry Association
3-2-4 Kasumigaseki, Chiyoda-ku, Tokyo 100-0013
Tel: +81 3 3519 2166
Fax: +81 3 3580 0764
Email: tedmine@jcia-net.or.jp

Mr. Seiichi Minamizuka

General Manager Plant Coordination
Group International Trade Administration Division
Japan Machinery Center for Trade and Investment
3-5-8 Shibakouen, Minato-ku, Tokyo 105-0011
Tel: +81 3 3431 9808
Fax: +81 3 3431 0509
Email: minamizuka@jmcti.or.jp

Mr. Daisuke Moriyama

Attorney
Criminal Bureau
Ministry of Justice
1-1-1Kasumigaseki, Chiyoda-ku, Tokyo 100-8977
Tel: +81 3 3580 4111
Fax: +81 3 3592 7067
Email: dm010495@MOJ.go.jp

Ms. Hisako Motoyama

Policy Analyst
Development Finance and Environment Programme
Friends of the Earth Japan
3-17-24-2F, Mejiro Toshima-ku Tokyo 171-0031
Tel: +81 3 3951 1081
Fax: +81 3 3951 1084
Email: motoyama@foejapan.org

Mr. Kazuya Murahashi
International Business Promotion Division Manager
NEC Corporation
5-7-1 Shiba, Minato-ku, Tokyo 108-8001
Tel: +81 3 3798 6041
Fax: +81 3 3798 6057
Email: k-murahashi@bx.jp.nec.com

Mr. Hisao Nishimura
Senior Manager
General Administration Department
International Division
Kajima Corporation
2-7, Motoakasaka 1-Chome, Minato-Ku, Tokyo 107-8388
Tel: +81 3 3404 3311
Fax: +81 3 3470 1444, 1445

Mr. Toru Oda
Manager
Toyota Motor Corporation
1 Toyotacyo, Toyota-shi Aichi 471-8571
Tel: +81 565 23 1641
Fax: +81 565 23 5714
Email: toru_oda@mail.toyota.co.jp

Mr. Hidehiro Okayama
Manager in Chief International Division
The Japan Chamber of Commerce and Industry
3-2-2 Marunouchi, Chiyoda-ku, Tokyo 100-0005
Tel: +81 3 3283 7605
Fax: +81 3 3216 6497
Email: hokayama@tokyo-cci.or.jp

Mr. Minoru O'uchi
Professor of Political Science
Graduate School of International Political Economy
Shu Mei University
1-1 Daigaku-Machi, Yachiyo-cho, Chiba 276-0063
Tel: +81 474 88 2111
Fax: +81 474 88 8290
Email: Ik8m-oouc@asahi-net.or.jp

Mr. Eiji Oyamada
Adjunct Assistant Professor
Institute of Development Management and Governance
University of the Philippines
Tel: +81 45 822 5979
Fax: +81 45 822 5979
Email: eiji_oyamada@hotmail.com

Ms. Emiko Ray
Public Management Consultant
Sunny Court 405
2-7-3 Suidou, Bunkyou-ku, Tokyo 112-0005
Tel: +81 90 1250 0426
Fax: +81 3 5981 6228
Email: emikoray@hotmail.com

Mr. Fumihiko Saito
Director and General Counsel
IBM Japan, Limited
3-2-12 Roppongi, Minato-ku, Tokyo 106-8111
Tel: +81 3 5563 3590
Fax: +81 3 5563 4882
Email: fsaito@jp.ibm.com

Mr. Soichiro Sakuma
Head of Legal Department
Nippon Steel Corporation
2-6-3 Otemachi, Chiyoda-ku, Tokyo 100-8071
Tel: +81 3 3275 5479
Fax: +81 3 3275 5984
Email: sakuma.soichiro@hg.nsc.co.jp

Mr. Hirotake Satoh
Official
Regional Policy Division
Asian and Oceanian Affairs Bureau
Ministry of Foreign Affairs
Shiba Koen 2-11-1, Minato-Ku, Tokyo 105-8519
Tel: +81 3 3580 3311
Fax: +81 3 3581 9470

Mr. Kuniji Shibahara
Professor
Gakushuin University
1-5-1 Mejiro, Toshima-ku, Tokyo 171-8588
Tel: +81 3 3986 0221
Fax: +81 3 5992 1006
Email: 19980056@gakushuin.ac.jp

Ms. Miki Shigenobu
Legal Division
Toyota Motor Corporation
1-4-18 Kouraku, Bunkyou-ku, Tokyo 112-8701
Tel: +81 3 5800 7482
Fax: +81 3 3817 9016
Email: m_shigenobu@mail.toyota.co.jp

Mr. Eiichi Shimomura
Deputy General Manager
Legal Department
Nissho Iwai Corporation
2-3-1 Daiba, Minato-ku, Tokyo 135-8655
Tel: +81 3 5520 2746
Fax: +81 3 5520 2724
Email: shimomura.eiichi@nisshoiwai.co.jp

Mr. Katsumi Shimomura
Daito Bunka University
Graduate School (Politics)
16-15 Takashimadaira 7-chome, Itabashi-ku, Tokyo 175-0082
Tel: +81 3 3975 8680
Fax: +81 3 3975 8680
Email: crown@tkg.att.ne.jp

Mr. Ping Ling Soh
Guest Researcher
Asahi Shimbun Asia Network
5-3-2 Tukiji, Chuuou-ku, Tokyo 104-8011
Tel: +81 3 5541 8464
Fax: +81 3 5541 8880
Email: aan@mx.asahi-np.co

Mr. Tsutomu Sugiura
Deputy Director
Marubeni Research Institute
Marubeni Corporation
1-4-2 Ootemachi, Chiyoda-ku, Tokyo 100-8088
Tel: +81 3 3282 4153
Fax: +81 3 3282 7492
Email: Sugiura-T@marubeni.com

Mr. Kazuo Takagi
Deputy Director
Asahi Shimbun Asia Network
Tel: +81 3 5541 8464
Fax: +81 3 5541 8880
Email: aan@mx.asahi-ne.co.jp

Mr. Masatoshi Tsuchiya
Manager
Legal and Intellectual Property Group Legal and International Department
Japan Electronics and Information Technology Industries association
Mitsuikaijyo Annex Building 3F
3-11 Kandasurugadai, Chiyoda-ku, Tokyo 101-0062
Tel: +81 3 3518 6432
Fax: +81 3 3295 8727
Email: m-tsuchiya@jeita.or.jp

Mr. Yoichiro Ueno
National Personnel Authority, Senior International Affairs Officer
1-1-1 Kasumigaseki, Chiyoda-ku, Tokyo 100-8913
Tel: +81 3 3501 1067
Fax: +81 3 3580 6092
Email: ueno-yoichiro@jinji.go.jp

Mr. Toru Umeda
Professor
Reitaku University
2-1-1 Hikarigaoka, Kashiwa-shi, Chiba 277-8686
Tel: +81 471 69 3978
Fax: +81 471 69 3978
Email: umeda@reitaku-u.ac.jp

Mr. Hirokazu Urata
Attorney
Criminal Bureau
Ministry of Justice
1-1-1 Kasumigaseki, Chiyoda-ku, Tokyo 100-8977
Tel: +81 3 3580 4111
Fax: +81 3 3592 7063
Email: hu010259@MOJ.go.jp

Ms. Kazumi Wada
Section Chief
Ministry of Public Management, Home Affairs, Posts and
Telecommunications
Minister's Secretariat, Policy Planning Division
Shiba Koen 2-11-1, Minato-Ku, Tokyo 105-8519
Tel: +81 3 5253 5156
Fax: +81 3 5253 5160
Email: k.wada@soumu.go.jp

Mr. Naoyuki I Wai
Attorney
Ministry of Foreign Affairs
Shiba Koen 2-11-1, Minato-Ku, Tokyo 105-8519
Tel: +81 3 3580 3311 ext. 3073
Fax: +81 3 35809319
Email: naoyuki.iwai@mofa.go.jp

Mr. Takeshi Yasuda
Deputy Manager
Global Capital Markets Group
Debt Capital Market Department
Nomura Securities Co., Ltd.
Urbannet Otemachi Building
2-2-2, Otemachi, Chiyoda-ku, Tokyo 100-8130
Tel: +81 3 3271 1047
Fax: +81 3 3271 5650
Email: yasuda-0f1p@jp.nomura.com

Ms. Satoko Yasuda
National Personnel Agency
International Affairs Officers
1-1-1 Kasumigaseki, Chiyoda-ku, Tokyo 100-8913
Tel: +81 3 3501 1067
Fax: +81 3 3580 6092
Email: yasudasat@jinji.go.jp

Mr. Junichiro Yoshino
Corporate Ethics Division Manager
NEC Corporation
5-7-1 Shiba, Minato-ku, Tokyo 108-8001
Tel: +81 3 3798 6194
Fax: +81 3 3798 6319
Email: j-yoshino@cb.jp.nec.com

KAZAKHSTAN

Mr. Anuarbek Akhmetov
Third Secretary
Embassy of the Republic of Kazakhstan in Japan
5-9-8 Himonya, Meguro-ku
Tokyo 152-0003, Japan
Tel: +81 3 3791 5273
Fax: +81 3 3791 5279

Mr. Kim Georgiy
Advisor to the President of the Republic of Kazakhstan
Office of the President
Astana
Tel: +7 3172 151 116
Fax: +7 3172 327 274

Mr. Yerlan Kubashev
Second Secretary
Embassy of the Republic of Kazakhstan in Japan
5-9-8 Himonya, Meguro-ku, Tokyo 152-0003
Tel: +81 3 3791 5273
Fax: +81 3 3791 5279

KOREA, REPUBLIC OF

Mr. Geo-Sung Kim
Secretary General
Transparency International – Korea
#508, KEB, Yonji-Dong, Chongro-ku
Seoul 110-740
Tel: +82 2 708 5858
Fax: +82 2 708 5859
Email: gs@ti.or.kr

Mr. Hochul Kim
Public Prosecutor
Ministry of Justice
Government Complex, 1 Chungang-dong
Gwasheon-shi Gtunggi-do
Seoul 427 720
Tel: +82 2 503 4020
Fax: +82 2 2110 3309
Email: hk85@moj.go.kr

Mr. Jhungsoo Park
Research Director
Seoul Institute for Transparency
University of Seoul
90 Jeonnong-dong, Dongdaemon-gu
Seoul, 130-743
Tel: +822 2210 2855/2602
Fax: +822 2210 2858
Email: jpark@uos.ac.kr

Mr. Sang-Ok Park
Senior Prosecutor
Seoul High Public Prosecutor's Office
Ministry of Justice
1724 Seocho-Dong, Seocho-gu
Seoul 137-740
Tel: +82 2 530 3395
Fax: +82 2 530 3325
Email: jadepark1@yahoo.co.kr

Mr. Zusun Rhee
Research Coordinator Director
Korea Economic Research Institute
FKI Building, 28-1 Yoido-Dong
Yeongdungpo-Ku , Seoul 150-756
Tel: +822 3771 0038
Fax: +822 785 0270
Email: zrhee@keri.org

Mr. Young-son Shin
Director, Inspection & Investigation Bureau
Office of the Prime Minister
77 Sejong-Ro, Jongro-ku
Seoul
Tel: + 82 2 3703 3831
Fax: + 82 2 723 1966
Email: sys7@opc.go.kr

Mr. Sangpo Suh
Deputy Director, Economic Organizations Division
Ministry of Foreign Affairs and Trade
77, Sejong-ro, Jong-Gu
Seoul 110-760
Tel: +82 2 720 2330
Fax: +82 2 722 7818
Email: spshuh93@mofat.go.kr

KYRGYZ REPUBLIC

Mr. Asylbek Bolotbaev
Head of Civil Service Unit
Head of the Commission Secretariat on Ethics
President Administration
Bishkek, House of Government
Tel: +996 312 664 162
Fax: +996 312 218 627
Email: dss-adm@mail.gov.kg

Ms. Tolekan Ismailova
Coalition of NGO's for Democracy and Civil Society
37/29 Ibraimova St.,
Bishkek 720021
Tel: +996 312 680972
Fax: +996 312 681216
Email: coalitionngo@infotel.kg

LAO PDR

Mr. Langsy Sibounheung
Vice Chairman of State Management Inspection Authority
Prime Minister's Office
Office KM6 Vientiane
Tel: +856 21 412 484
Fax: +856 21 412 869

MALAYSIA

Mr. Auni Abdullah
Counsellor
Embassy of Malaysia in Tokyo, Japan
20-16, Nanpeidai-cho, Shibuya-Ku 150
Tel: +81 3 3476 3840
Fax: +81 3 3476 4971

Mr. Tunku Abdul Aziz
Vice Chairman of Board of Directors – Transparency International
President of TI-Malaysia
2-2-49 Wisma Rampai, Jalan 34/26
Taman Sri Rampai, Setapak
55300 Kuala Lumpur
Tel: +603 4819 9131
Fax: +603 4143 5968
Email: info@transparency.org

Dato' Haji Nordin Bin Ismail
Director and Investigation
Anti-Corruption Agency of Malaysia
Headquarters, Level 2, Block D6, P.O. Box 6000
Federal Government Administration Centre, 62502 Putrajaya

Tel: +603 8886 7000
Fax: +603 8888 9489

Dato' Zulkipli' Bin Mat Noor
Director General
Anti-Corruption Agency of Malaysia
Headquarters, Level 7, Block D6, P.O. Box 6000
Federal Government Administration Centre, 62502 Putrajaya
Tel: +603 8886 7004
Fax: +603 8888 9562
Email: bprupkd@po.jaring.my

Mr. Yaacob Bin Md. Sam
Senior Federal Counsel
Legal and Prosecution
Anti-Corruption Agency of Malaysia
Headquarters, Level 7, Block D6, P.O. Box 6000
Federal Government Administration Centre, 62502 Putrajaya
Tel: +603 8886 7000
Fax: +603 8888 9562
Email: yaacobms@bpr.gov.my

MEXICO

Mr. Armando Lopez Trujillo
Second Secretary
International Cooperation
Education, Science and technology
Embassy of Mexico
2-15-1 Nagata-cho, Chiyoda-ku, Tokyo 100-0014
Japan
Tel: +81 3 3581 1131
Fax: +81 3 3581 4058
Email: embeduca@md.neweb.ne.jp

MONGOLIA

Ambassador Zambyn Batjargal
Embassy of Mongolia to Japan
21-4 Kamiyama-cho, Shibuya-ku
Tokyo 150, Japan

Tel: +81 3 3469 2216
Fax: +81 3 3469 2088
Email: embmong@gol.com

NEPAL

Mr. Surya Nath Upadhyay
Chief Commissioner
Commission for the Investigation of Abuse and Authority
KMA 1, 488 Gimattekula Height
Dillibazar, Kathmandu
Tel: +977 1 262 378
Fax: +977 1 262 930
Email: akhtiyar@ntc.net.np

NEW ZEALAND

Mr. John Mataira
First Secretary
New Zealand Embassy
20-40 Kuniyama-cho, Shihuya-ku
Tokyo 150-0047, Japan
Tel: +81 3 3467 2271
Fax: +81 3 3467 6843

PAKISTAN

Mr. Nooruddin Ahmed
Transparency International – Pakistan
83-Q Khalid bib Waleed Bock-2
PECH Society
Karachi
Tel: +92 21 455 2438
Fax: +92 21 455 9152
Email: Ti-pak@khi.paknet.com.pk

Lt. Gen. Munir Hafiez
Chairman
National Accountability Bureau
Chief Executive's Secretariat
Constitution Avenue, Islamabad

Tel: +9251 920 7012
Fax: +9251 920 1821
Email: info@nab.gov.pk

Rear Admiral Obaid Sadiq
Head
Regional Accountability Bureau,
RMC Hostel No. 3 Chaklala Road, Rawalpindi
Tel: +9251 595 1961
Fax: +9251 595 1962
Email: nab@apollo.net.pk

PAPUA NEW GUINEA

Mr. Mathew Yuangu
Director of Governance, Law, Justice and International Affairs
Department of Prime Minister and National Executive Council
P.O. Box 639, Waigani
Tel: +327 6711/6741
Fax: +327 6755
Email: myuangu@hotmail.com

PHILIPPINES

Ms. Sheila Coronel
Executive Director
Philippine Center for Investigative Journalism
3rd Floor, Criselda II Building
107 Scout de Guia, Quezon City 1104
Tel: +632 410 4768/69
Fax: +632 410 1346
Email: scoronel@pcij.org

Mr. Jaime Guerrero
Chief of Staff
Office of the Vice-President
PICC Building, CCP Complex
Roxas Boulevard, Pasay City
Tel: +632 551 3897
Fax: +632 831 2618
Email: chiefovp@yahoo.com

Mr. Joseph Michael Quiazon
Director, Risk Consulting
Arthur Andersen
6760 Ayala avenue, Makati City, 1226
Tel: +632 894 8330
Fax: +632 812 6790
Email: joseph.m.quiazon@ph.andersen.com

Mr. Luis Teodoro, Jr.
Associate Director
Center for Media Freedom and Responsibility
130 H.V. de la Costa, Makati City 1227
Tel: +632 893 1314
Fax: +632 840 0889
Email: cmfr@surfshop.net.ph or teodoro@info.com.ph

SAMOA

Ms. Lusia Sefo Leau
Deputy Financial Secretary
Treasury Department
Private Mailbag
Apia
Tel: +685 34333
Fax: +685 21312
Email: lucia@samoa.ws

SINGAPORE

Dr. Gillian Koh
Research Fellow
The Institute of Policy Studies
1 Hon Sui Sen Drive
Tel: +65 775 1194
Fax: +65 776 7907
Email: gillian_koh@ips.org.sg

Mr. Chua Cher Yak
Director
Corrupt Practices Investigation Bureau
150 Cantonment Road

Singapore 089762
Tel: + 65 324 3680
Fax: + 65 323 5459
Email: *CHUA_cher_yak@cpib.gov.sg*

Prof. Jon S.T. Quah
Professor of Political Science
Department of Political Science
Faculty of Arts and Social Science
National University of Singapore
AS1, 4ᵗʰ Level, 11 Arts Link
Singapore 117570
Tel: +65 874 6229 /3971
Fax: +65 779 6815
Email: *polqst@nus.edu.sg*

SLOVAK REPUBLIC

Ms. Monika Smolova
Office of Deputy Prime Minister for Economic Affairs
Central Coordinating Unit for the Fight Against Corruption
Namestie Slobody 1
813 70 Bratislava 1
Tel: +421 2 57 295 105
Fax: +421 1 52 497 530
Email: *monika.smolova@government.gov.sk*

Mr. Mario Vircik
Office of Deputy Prime Minister for Economic Affairs
Central Coordinating Unit for the Fight Against Corruption
Namestie Slobody 1
813 70 Bratislava 1
Tel: +421 2 57 295 383
Email: *mario.vircik@government.gov.sk*

SWITZERLAND

Ms. Gemma Aiolfi
Assistant to the President of the OECD Working Group on Bribery
University of Basel
Maiengasse 51
CH-4056 Basel
Tel: +41 61 267 2538
Fax: +41 61 267 2549
Email: gemma.aiolfi@unibas.ch

Prof. Mark Pieth
Professor for Criminal Law
University of Basel, Switzerland
President
OECD Working Group on Bribery in International Business Transactions
Maiengasse 51
CH-4056 Basel
Tel: +41 61 267 2538
Fax: +41 61 267 2549
Email: mark.pieth@unibas.ch

TAIPEI, CHINA

Dr. Szu-chien Hsu
Assistant Research Fellow
Institute of International Relations, NCCU
64 Wan Shou Road
Taipei 116
Tel: +886 2 2939 4921 ext. 391
Fax: +886 2 2738 7061
Email: sh81@nccu.edu.tw

Dr. Chilik Yu
Associate Professor
Shih Hsin University
No. 1, Lane 17, Mu-Cha Rd, Sec. 1
Taipei
Tel: +886 2 2236 8225 ext. 3461
Fax: +886 2 2236 3325
Email: cyu@cc.shu.edu.tw

THAILAND

Mr. Chitchai Panichapat
Deputy Secretary General
National Counter Corruption Commission
Pitsanuloke Road, Dusit
Bangkok 10300
Tel: +662 282 3161 5 ext. 411
Fax: +662 281 8467
Email: prachuabmoh1@hotmail.com

Mr. Nitiphan Prachuabmoh
Official
Bureau of Planning and Development
National Counter Corruption Commission
Pitsanuloke Road, Dusit
Bangkok 10300
Tel: +662 282 3161 5 ext. 411
Fax: +662 281 8467
Email: prachuabmoh1@hotmail.com

Ms. Laura Thornton
Senior Program Manager
The National Democratic Institute for International Affairs
170c Soi Prasarnmitr 3
Sukhumvit Bangkok
Tel: +662 261 4604
Fax: +662 664 0471
Email: Laura@mozart.inet.co.th

Ms. Anukansai Kanokkan
Program Officer
Transparency International – Thailand
c/o Center for Philanthropy and Civil Society
National Institute of Development Administration
Seri-Thai Road, Klongchan, Bangkapi
Bangkok 10240
Tel: +662 377 7206/662 378 1284
Fax: +662 374 7399
Email: kanukansai@hotmail.com

UNITED KINGDOM

Mr. Phil Mason
Anti-Corruption Coordinator
Governance Department
Department of International Development
94 Victoria Street
London SW1E 5JL
Tel: +44 207 917 0171
Fax: +44 207 917 0074
Email: ps-mason@dfid.gov.uk

UNITED STATES

Ms. Lisa Dickieson
Director, Asia Law Initiative
American Bar Association
740 15th Street, N.W.
Washington, D.C. 20005
Tel: +1 202 662 8687
Fax: +1 202 662 1741
Email: DickiesL@staff.abanet.org

Mr. David Luna
Special Advisor, Anticorruption & Governance
U.S. State Department
2201 C Street
Washington, D.C. 20520
Tel: +1 202 736 4556
Fax: +1 202 736 4515
Email: lunadm@state.gov

VANUATU

Mr. Jimmy Andeng
Acting Director General
Ministry of Comprehensive Reform Program
PMB 083, Port Vila
Tel: +678 24845
Fax: +678 25481
Email: Jimmyandeng@hotmail.com

Mrs. Marie-Noelle Ferrieux Patterson
President
Transparency International Vanuatu
P.O. Box 355
Port Vila
Tel: +678 22231/23441
Fax: +678 25660
Email: patclan@vanuatu.com.vu

VIETNAM

Ms. Trinh Nhu Hoa
Specialist
Vietnam State Inspectorate
International Affairs, Vietnam State Inspectorate
220 Doi Can Street, Hanoi
Tel: +844 832 5786
Fax: +844 804 8493
Email: ttnn@hn.vnn.vn

Mr. Nguyen Huu Loc
Chief Inspector
Head of Vietnam State Inspectorate
International Affairs, Vietnam State Inspectorate
220 Doi Can Street, Hanoi
Tel: +844 832 5786
Fax: +844 804 8493

Mr. Le Luong Minh
Deputy Director
Ministry of Foreign Affairs
5 Chu Van An Street, Hanoi
Tel: +844 199 3352
Fax: +844 199 3115

H.E. Mr. Ta Huu Thanh
Minister, Inspector General
Vietnam State Inspectorate
220 Doi Can Street, Hanoi
Tel: +844 832 5786
Fax: +844 804 8493
Email: ttnn@hn.vnn.vn

INTERNATIONAL ORGANIZATIONS

ASIAN DEVELOPMENT BANK
6 ADB Avenue, Mandaluyong City
0401 Metro Manila
P.O. Box 789, 0980 Manila, Philippines
Tel: +632 632 4444
Fax: +632 636 2444

Mr. Shoji Nishimoto
Director
Strategy and Policy Department
Tel: +632 632 6550
Email: snishimoto@adb.org

Mr. Bart Edes
Senior External Relations Officer
Office of External Relations
Tel: +632 632 5870
Email: bedes@adb.org

Mr. Michael Stevens
Senior Audit Specialist
Office of the General Auditor
Tel: +632 632 5049
Email: mstevens@adb.org

Mr. Denis Osborne
Consultant
112 Dulwich Village
SE 21 7AQ
London, UK
Tel: +44 0 20 8693 7100
Fax: +44 0 20 8693 0906
Email: do@governance.org.uk

ADB– Indonesia Resident Mission

Mr. Staffan Synnerstrom
Senior Governance Advisor
Gedung BRI II, 7ᵗʰ Floor
Jl. Jend Sudirman Kav. 44-46
Jakarta 10350A
Tel: +62 21 251 2721
Fax: +62 21 251 2749
Email: ssynnerstrom@adb.org

Asian Development Bank Institute
8/F Kasumigaseki Building
2-5 Kasumigaseki 3 Chome
Chiyoda-ku, Tokyo 100, Japan
Tel: +813 3593 5500
Fax::+813 3593 5571
Email: info@adbi.org

Dr. Masaru Yoshitomi
Dean
Email: myoshitomi@adbi.org

Dr. Raj Chhikara
Senior Capacity Building Specialist
Email: rchhikara@adbi.org

Dr. Terrence Morrison
Senior Training and Learning Methods Specialist
Email: tmorrison@adbi.org

ADB– Japanese Representative Office
Yamato Seimei Building
1-7 Uchi Uchisaiwaicho 1-Chome
Chiyoda-ku, Tokyo 100-0011
Tel: +813 3504 3160
Fax: +813 3504 3165
Email: adbjro@adb.org

Mr. Koichi Ishikura
Senior Liaison Officer
Email: kishikura@adb.org

Mr. Jungsoo Lee
Director
Email: jungsoolee@adb.org

THE ASIA FOUNDATION

Mr. Gavin Tritt
The Asia Foundation
Assistant Representative, Philippines
P.O. Box 7072
Domestic Airport Post Office
Pasay City, Philippines
Tel: +63 2 851 1466
Fax::+632 853 0474
Email: gavin@asiafound.org.ph

ORGANISATION FOR ECONOMIC CO-OPERATION AND DEVELOPMENT
2, rue André-Pascal
F-75775 Paris Cedex 16
France
Tel: +33 1 4524 1855
Fax: +33 1 4430 6307

Mr. Janos Bertok
Principal Administrator
Division on Governance and the Role of the State
Public Management Service
Tel: +33 1 4524 9357
Email: janos.bertok@oecd.org

Ms. Wendy Prince-Lagoutte
Administrative Assistant
Anti-Corruption Division
Directorate for Financial, Fiscal and Enterprise Affairs
Tel: +33 1 4524 1810
Fax: +33 1 4430 6307
Email: wendy.prince-lagoutte@oecd.org

Mrs. Hélène Gadriot-Renard
Head
Division on Governance and the Role of the State
Public Management Service
Tel: +33 1 4524 9460
Email: helene.gadriot-renard@oecd.org

OECD TOKYO CENTER
3rd Floor, Nippon Press Center Building
2-2-1 Uchisaiwaicho, Chiyoda-Ku
Tokyo 100-0011 Japan
Tel: +81 3 5532 0021
Fax: +81 3 5532 0036

Mr. Makoto Yamanaka
Head
Tel: +81 3 3586 2016
Fax: +81 3 3586 2298
Email: makoto.yamanaka@oecd.org

Ms. Noriko Mimura
Public Affairs Officer
Tel: +81 3 3586 2016
Fax: +81 3 3586 2298
Email: noriko.mimura@oecd.org

Ms. Junko Ohashi
Commercial Assistant
Tel: +81 3 3586 2016
Fax: +81 3 3586 2298
Email: junko.ohashi@oecd.org

PACIFIC BASIN ECONOMIC COUNCIL-JAPAN
c/o The Japan and Tokyo Chambers of Commerce & Industry
2-2 Marunouchi 3-Chome, Chiyoda-ku
Tokyo 100-0005, Japan
Tel: +81 3 3283 7608
Fax: +81 3 3216 6497
Email: pbec-jpn@tokyo-cci.or.jp

Mr. Shigeo Hashimoto
Director General

Mr. Masao Akamatsu
Project Manager

Mr. Thomas Arai
Chairman
Systems International

Mr. Kazuya Murahashi
Manager of International Business Promotion Division
NEC Corporation

Mr. Tomoaki Oigawa
Assistant Manager, International Division
Tokyo Chamber of Commerce and Industry

Mr. Akiko Saito
International Division
Tokyo Chamber of Commerce and Industry

PACIFIC BASIN ECONOMIC COUNCIL

Mr. Michael Davies
Chair of Transparency Committee
2300 Meadowvale Blvd.
Mississauga, ON L5N 5P9
Canada
Tel: +1 905 858 5231
Fax: +1 905 858 5234
Email: michael.davies@corporate.ge.com

Mr. Alex Jampel
Pacific Basin Economic Council Japan
Chun, Kerr, Dodd, Beaman & Wong
Hawaii Tower, 9th Floor
745 Fort Street
Honolulu, Hawaii 96813-3815
Tel: +1 808 528 8200
Fax: +1 808 528 8288
Email: ajampel@ckdbw.com

Mr. Robert Lees
Secretary General
Pacific Basin Economic Council
900 Fort Street, suite 1080, Honolulu
Hawaii 96813
Tel: +1 808 521 9044
Fax: +1 808 521 8530
Email: boblees@pbec.org

Mr. Steve Olson
Deputy Secretary General
Pacific Basin Economic Council
900 Fort Street, suite 1080, Honolulu
Hawaii 96813
Tel: +1 808 521 9044
Fax: +1 808 521 8530
Email: steve@pbec.org

TRANSPARENCY INTERNATIONAL, INTERNATIONAL SECRETARIAT
97-99 Otto Suhr Allee
10585 Berlin

Ms. Margit Van Ham
Executive Director
Tel: +49 30 343 8200
Fax: +49 30 3470 3912
Email: mvham@transparency.org

Ms. Lisa Prevenslik-Takeda
Programme Officer
South East/East Asia
Tel: +49 30 3438 2062
Fax: +49 30 3470 3912
Email: lptakeda@transparency.org

UNITED NATIONS DEVELOPMENT PROGRAMME-TOKYO
UNDP Tokyo Office
UNU Bldg. 8F, Jingumae 5-53-70
Shibuya-ku, Tokyo 150-0001
Tel: +81-3-5467-4751
Fax: +81-3-5467-4753

Ms. Yoko Iwasa
Email: yoko.iwasa@undp.org

Mr. Nicole Triplett
Email: nicole.triplett@undp.org

WORLD BANK-INDONESIA

Mr. Lateef Sarwar
Senior Advisor
World Bank Office - Jakarta
Jakarta Stock Exchange Building
Tower 2, 12th Floor
Jl. Jenderal Surdiman Kav. 52-53
Jakarta 12190
Tel: +62 21 52993000
Fax: +62 21 52993111
Email: klateef@worldbank.org

THE SECRETARIAT
ADB-OECD ANTI-CORRUPTION INITIATIVE FOR
ASIA-PACIFIC

OECD
Ms. Gretta Fenner
Manager, Anti-Corruption Initiative for Asia-Pacific
Anti-Corruption Division
Directorate for Financial, Fiscal and Enterprise Affairs
Tel: +33 1 45 2476 01
Fax: +33 1 44 3063 07
Email: gretta.fenner@oecd.org

Mr. Frédéric Wehrle

Co-ordinator, outreach Anti-Corruption Initiatives
Anti-Corruption Division
Directorate for Financial, Fiscal and Enterprise Affairs
Tel: +33 1 45 2418 55
Fax: +33 1 45 2478 52
Email: frederic.wehrle@oecd.org

ADB

Mr. Jak Jabes

Advisor for Governance
Governance and Regional Cooperation Division
Regional and Sustainable Development Department
Tel: +632 632 5749
Fax: +632 636 2193
Email: jjabes@adb.org

Ms. Marilyn Pizarro

Consultant
Governance and Regional Cooperation Division
Regional and Sustainable Development Department
Tel: +632 632 5917
Fax: +632 636 2193
Email: mpizarro@adb.org

ANTI-CORRUPTION ACTION PLAN FOR ASIA AND THE PACIFIC[1]

[1] Endorsed on 30 November 2001 in Tokyo, Japan by Bangladesh, Cook Islands, Fiji Islands, India, Indonesia, Japan, Republic of Korea, Kyrgyz Republic, Malaysia, Mongolia, Nepal, Pakistan, Papua New Guinea, Philippines, Samoa, Singapore, and Vanuatu. Kazakhstan endorsed the Action Plan on 22 May 2002. Other ADB member countries from Asia and the Pacific are invited to endorse the Action Plan. Other language versions of the Action Plan can be downloaded at: http://www.oecd.org/daf/ASIAcom/ActionPlan.htm

Preamble[2]

WE, governments of the Asia-Pacific region, building on objectives identified at the Manila Conference in October 1999 and subsequently at the Seoul Conference in December 2000;

CONVINCED that corruption is a widespread phenomenon which undermines good governance, erodes the rule of law, hampers economic growth and efforts for poverty reduction and distorts competitive conditions in business transactions;

ACKNOWLEDGING that corruption raises serious moral and political concerns and that fighting corruption is a complex undertaking and requires the involvement of all elements of society;

CONSIDERING that regional cooperation is critical to the effective fight against corruption;

RECOGNIZING that national anti-corruption measures can benefit from existing relevant regional and international instruments and good practices such as those developed by the countries in the region, the Asian Development Bank (ADB), the Asia-Pacific Economic Cooperation (APEC), the Financial Action Task Force on Money Laundering (FATF), the Organisation for Economic Co-operation and Development (OECD), the Pacific Basin Economic Council (PBEC), the United Nations and the World Trade Organization (WTO)[3].

---

[2] The Action Plan, together with its implementation plan, is a legally non-binding document which contains a number of principles and standards towards policy reform which interested governments of the region politically commit to implement on a voluntary basis.

[3] In particular: the 40 Recommendations of the FATF as supported by the Asia/Pacific Group on Money Laundering, the Anti-Corruption Policy of the ADB, the APEC Public Procurement Principles, the Basel Capital Accord of the Basel Committee on Banking

CONCUR, as governments of the region, in taking concrete and meaningful priority steps to deter, prevent and combat corruption at all levels, without prejudice to existing international commitments and in accordance with our jurisdictional and other basic legal principles;

WELCOME the pledge of representatives of the civil society and the business sector to promote integrity in business and in civil society activities and to support the governments of the region in their anti-corruption effort;

WELCOME the pledge made by donor countries and international organizations from outside and within the region to support the countries of the region in their fight against corruption through technical cooperation programmes.

Supervision, the OECD Convention on Combating Bribery of Foreign Public Officials in International Business Transactions and the Revised Recommendation, the OECD Council Recommendation on Improving Ethical Conduct in the Public Service, the OECD Principles on Corporate Governance, the PBEC Charter on Standards for Transactions between Business and Government, the United Nations Convention on Transnational Organized Crime and the WTO Agreement on Government Procurement.

Pillars of Action

I n order to meet the above objectives, participating governments in the region endeavour to take concrete steps under the following three pillars of action with the support, as appropriate, of ADB, OECD and other donor organizations and countries:

PILLAR 1—DEVELOPING EFFECTIVE AND TRANSPARENT SYSTEMS FOR PUBLIC SERVICE

Integrity in Public Service

Establish systems of government hiring of public officials that assure openness, equity and efficiency and promote hiring of individuals of the highest levels of competence and integrity through:

- Development of systems for compensation adequate to sustain appropriate livelihood and according to the level of the economy of the country in question;
- Development of systems for transparent hiring and promotion to help avoid abuses of patronage, nepotism and favoritism, help foster the creation of an independent civil service, and help promote a proper balance between political and career appointments;
- Development of systems to provide appropriate oversight of discretionary decisions and of personnel with authority to make discretionary decisions; and
- Development of personnel systems that include regular and timely rotation of assignments to reduce insularity that would foster corruption.

Establish ethical and administrative codes of conduct that proscribe conflicts of interest, ensure the proper use of public resources, and promote the highest levels of professionalism and integrity through:

- Prohibitions or restrictions governing conflicts of interest;

- Systems to promote transparency through disclosure and/or monitoring of, for example, personal assets and liabilities;
- Sound administration systems which ensure that contacts between government officials and business services users, notably in the area of taxation, customs and other corruption-prone areas, are free from undue and improper influence.
- Promotion of codes of conduct taking due account of the existing relevant international standards as well as each country's traditional cultural standards, and regular education, training and supervision of officials to ensure proper understanding of their responsibilities; and
- Measures which ensure that officials report acts of corruption and which protect the safety and professional status of those who do.

Accountability and Transparency

Safeguard accountability of public service through effective legal frameworks, management practices and auditing procedures through:

- Measures and systems to promote fiscal transparency;
- Adoption of existing relevant international standards and practices for regulation and supervision of financial institutions;
- Appropriate auditing procedures applicable to public administration and the public sector, and measures and systems to provide timely public reporting on performance and decision making;
- Appropriate transparent procedures for public procurement that promote fair competition and deter corrupt activity, and adequate simplified administration procedures;
- Enhancing institutions for public scrutiny and oversight;
- Systems for information availability including on issues such as application processing procedures, funding of political parties and electoral campaigns and expenditure; and
- Simplification of the regulatory environment by abolishing overlapping, ambiguous or excessive regulations that burden business.

PILLAR 2— STRETHENING ANTI-BRIBERY ACTIONS AND PROMOTING INTEGRITY IN BUSINESS OPERATIONS

Effective Prevention, Investigation and Prosecution

Take effective measures to actively combat bribery by:

- Ensuring the existence of legislation with dissuasive sanctions which effectively and actively combat the offence of bribery of public officials;
- Ensuring the existence and effective enforcement of anti-money laundering legislation that provide for substantial criminal penalties for the laundering of the proceeds of corruption and crime consistent with the law of each country;
- Ensuring the existence and enforcement of rules to ensure that bribery offences are thoroughly investigated and prosecuted by competent authorities; these authorities should be empowered to order that bank, financial or commercial records be made available or be seized and that bank secrecy be lifted;
- Strengthening of investigative and prosecutorial capacities by fostering inter-agency cooperation, by ensuring that investigation and prosecution are free from improper influence and have effective means for gathering evidence, by protecting those persons helping the authorities in combating corruption, and by providing appropriate training and financial resources; and
- Strengthening bi- and multilateral cooperation in investigations and other legal proceedings by developing systems which – in accordance with domestic legislation – enhance (i) effective exchange of information and evidence, (ii) extradition where expedient, and (iii) cooperation in searching and discovering of forfeitable assets as well as prompt international seizure and repatriation of these forfeitable assets.

Corporate Responsibility and Accountability

Take effective measures to promote corporate responsibility and accountability on the basis of existing relevant international standards through:

- Promotion of good corporate governance which would provide for adequate internal company controls such as codes of conduct, the establishment of channels for communication, the protection of employees reporting corruption, and staff training;
- The existence and the effective enforcement of legislation to eliminate any indirect support of bribery such as tax deductibility of bribes;

- The existence and thorough implementation of legislation requiring transparent company accounts and providing for effective, proportionate and dissuasive penalties for omissions and falsifications for the purpose of bribing a public official, or hiding such bribery, in respect of the books, records, accounts and financial statements of companies; and

- Review of laws and regulations governing public licenses, government procurement contracts or other public undertakings, so that access to public sector contracts could be denied as a sanction for bribery of public officials.

PILLAR 3 – SUPPORTING ACTIVE PUBLIC INVOLVEMENT

Public Discussion of Corruption

Take effective measures to encourage public discussion of the issue of corruption through:

- Initiation of public awareness campaigns at different levels;
- Support of nongovernmental organizations that promote integrity and combat corruption by, for example, raising awareness of corruption and its costs, mobilizing citizen support for clean government, and documenting and reporting cases of corruption; and
- Preparation and/or implementation of education programs aimed at creating an anti-corruption culture.

Access to Information

Ensure that the general public and the media have freedom to receive and impart public information and in particular information on corruption matters in accordance with domestic law and in a manner that would not compromise the operational effectiveness of the administration or, in any other way, be detrimental to the interest of governmental agencies and individuals, through:

- Establishment of public reporting requirements for justice and other governmental agencies that include disclosure about efforts to promote integrity and accountability and combat corruption; and
- Implementation of measures providing for a meaningful public right of access to appropriate information.

Public Participation

Encourage public participation in anticorruption activities, in particular through:

- Cooperative relationships with civil society groups such as chambers of commerce, professional associations, nongovernment organizations (NGOs), labor unions, housing associations, the media, and other organizations;
- Protection of whistleblowers; and
- Involvement of NGOs in monitoring of public sector programmes and activities.

Implementation

In order to implement these three pillars of action, participating governments of the region concur with the attached Implementation Plan and will endeavour to comply with its terms.

Participating governments of the region further commit to widely publicize the Action Plan throughout government agencies and the media and, in the framework of the Steering Group Meetings, to meet and to assess progress in the implementation of the actions contained in the Action Plan.

Implementation Plan

Introduction

The Action Plan contains legally non-binding principles and standards towards policy reform which participating governments of the Asia-Pacific region (hereinafter: participating governments) voluntarily commit to implement in order to combat corruption and bribery in a coordinated and comprehensive manner and thus contribute to development, economic growth and social stability. Although the Action Plan describes policy objectives that are currently relevant to the fight against corruption in Asia and the Pacific, it remains open to ideas and partners. Updates of the Action Plan will be the responsibility of the Steering Group.

This section describes the implementation of the Action Plan. Taking into account national conditions, implementation will draw upon existing instruments and good practices developed by countries of the region and international organizations such as the Asian Development Bank (ADB), the Asia-Pacific Economic Cooperation (APEC), the Organisation for Economic Co-operation and Development (OECD) and the United Nations.

Core principles of Implementation

The implementation of the Action Plan will be based upon two core principles: i) establishing a mechanism by which overall reform progress can be promoted and assessed; ii) providing specific and practical assistance to governments of participating countries on key reform issues.

The implementation of the Action Plan will thus aims at offering participating countries regional and country-specific policy and institution-building support. This strategy will be tailored to policy priorities identified by participating countries and provide means by which participating countries and partners can assess progress and measure the achieved results.

Identifying Country Priorities

While the Action Plan recalls the need to fight corruption and lays out overall policy objectives, it acknowledges that the situation in each country of the region may be specific.

To address these differences and target country-specific technical assistance, each participating country will endeavour, in consultation with the Secretariat of the Initiative, to identify priority reform areas which would fall under any of the three pillars, and aim to implement these in a workable timeframe.

The first consultation on these priorities will take place in the framework of the Tokyo Conference, immediately after the formal endorsement of the Action Plan. Subsequent identification of target areas will be done in the framework of the periodical meetings of the Steering Group that will be set up to review progress in the implementation of the Action Plan's three pillars.

Reviewing Progress in the Reform Process

Real progress will primarily come from the efforts of the governments of each participating country supported by the business sector and civil society. In order to promote emulation, increase country responsibilities and target bilateral and international technical assistance, a mechanism will be established by which overall progress can be promoted and reviewed.

The review process will focus on the priority reform areas selected by participating countries. In addition, there will be a thematic discussion dealing with issues of specific, cross-regional importance as identified by the Steering Group.

Review of progress will be based on self-assessment reports by participating countries. The review process will use a procedure of plenary review by the Steering Group to take stock of each country's implementation progress.

Providing Assistance to the Reform Process

While governments of participating countries have primary responsibility for addressing corruption related problems, the regional and international community as well as civil society and the business sector have a key role to play in supporting countries' reform efforts.

Donor countries and other assistance providers supporting the Action Plan will endeavour to provide the assistance required to enhance the capacity of participating countries to achieve progress in the priority areas and to meet the overall policy objectives of the Action Plan.

Participating governments of the region will endeavour, in consultation with the Initiative's Secretariat, to make known their specific assistance requirements in each of the selected priority areas and will cooperate with the assistance providers in the elaboration, organization and implementation of programmes.

Providers of technical assistance will support participating governments' anti-corruption efforts by building upon programmes and initiatives already in place, avoiding duplications and facilitating, whenever possible, joint ventures. The Secretariat will continue to support this process through the Initiative's web site (www.oecd.org/daf/ASIAcom) which provides information on existing and planned assistance programmes and initiatives.

Mechanisms

Country Representatives

To facilitate the implementation of the Action Plan, each participating government in the region will designate a contact person. This government representative will have sufficient authority as well as adequate staff support and resources to oversee the fulfillment of the policy objectives of the Action Plan on behalf of his/her government.

Regional Steering Group

A Steering Group will be established and meet back-to-back with the Initiative's annual conferences to review progress achieved by participating countries in implementing the Action Plan. It will be composed of the government representatives and national experts on the technical issues discussed during the respective meeting as well as representatives of the Initiative's Secretariat and Advisory Group (see below).

The Steering Group will meet on an annual basis and serve three main purposes: (i) to review progress achieved in implementing each country's priorities; (ii) to serve as a forum for the exchange of experience and for addressing cross-regional issues that arise in connection with the implementation of the policy objectives laid out in the Action Plan; and (iii) to promote a dialogue with representatives of the international community, civil society and the business sector in order to mobilize donor support.

Consultations in the Steering Group will take place on the day preceding the Initiative's annual meeting. This shall allow the Steering Group to report on progress achieved in the implementation of the policy objectives laid out in the Action Plan, present regional good practices and enlarge support for anti-corruption efforts among ADB regional member countries.

Secretariat

The ADB and the OECD will act as the Secretariat of the Initiative and, as such, carry out day-to-day management. The role of the Secretariat also includes providing assistance to participating governments in preparing their self-review reports. For this purpose, in-country missions by the Secretariat will be organized when necessary.

Advisory Group

The Secretariat will be assisted by an informal Advisory Group whose responsibility will be to help mobilize resources for technical assistance programmes and advise on priorities for the implementation of the Action Plan. The Group will be composed of donor countries and international donor organizations as well as representatives of civil society and the business sector, such as the Pacific Basin Economic Council (PBEC) and Transparency International (TI), actively involved in the implementation of the Action Plan.

Funding

Technical assistance programmes and policy advice in support of government reforms as well as capacity building in the business sector and civil society aiming at implementing the Action Plan will be financially supported by international organizations, governments and other parties from inside and outside the region actively supporting the Action Plan.